Diversifying Pedagogy in Early Childhood Teacher Preparation Programs

Diversifying Pedagogy in Early Childhood Teacher Preparation Programs

Edited by
Mari Riojas-Cortez

ROWMAN & LITTLEFIELD
Lanham • Boulder • New York • London

Published by Rowman & Littlefield
An imprint of The Rowman & Littlefield Publishing Group, Inc.
4501 Forbes Boulevard, Suite 200, Lanham, Maryland 20706
www.rowman.com

6 Tinworth Street, London, SE11 5AL, United Kingdom

Copyright © 2021 by The Rowman & Littlefield Publishing Group, Inc.

All rights reserved. No part of this book may be reproduced in any form or by any electronic or mechanical means, including information storage and retrieval systems, without written permission from the publisher, except by a reviewer who may quote passages in a review.

British Library Cataloging in Publication Information Available

Library of Congress Cataloging-in-Publication Data

Names: Riojas-Cortez, Mari, editor.
Title: Diversifying pedagogy in early childhood teacher preparation programs / Edited by Mari Riojas-Cortez.
Description: Lanham : Rowman & Littlefield, [2021] | Includes bibliographical references. | Summary: "This book presents examples of faculty taking the lead to help preservice teachers understand the social injustices in aspects of early childhood education"—Provided by publisher.
Identifiers: LCCN 2021011771 (print) | LCCN 2021011772 (ebook) | ISBN 9781475860061 (cloth) | ISBN 9781475860078 (paperback) | ISBN 9781475860085 (epub)
Subjects: LCSH: Early childhood educators—Training of. | Early childhood education. | Critical pedagogy. | Multicultural education. | Mentoring in education. | Teachers—Professional relationships.
Classification: LCC LB1775.6 .D58 2021 (print) | LCC LB1775.6 (ebook) | DDC 372.21—dc23
LC record available at https://lccn.loc.gov/2021011771
LC ebook record available at https://lccn.loc.gov/2021011772

Contents

List of Figures	vii
Foreword	ix
Introduction	xi

1 Perceptions and Misconceptions: How Best to Prepare Early Childhood Teachers to Work with Dual Language Learners 1
Cristina Gillanders and Marlene Zepeda

2 Preparing Generalist Early Childhood Teachers to Work with Culturally and Linguistically Diverse Children Who Have Special Needs 19
Allegra Montemayor and Karen Walker

3 Preservice Teacher Confessions: "Why Should I Care about Parents?" 35
Tivy Nobles Whitlock

4 The Early Childhood Teacher Self-Reflection Model 47
Mari Riojas-Cortez and Tivy Nobles Whitlock

References	59
About the Editor and Contributors	71

List of Figures

Figure 1.1　Matrix of Pedagogical Competence of Early Educators Working with DLLs　15
Figure 4.1　Reflexive Process BEFORE the model　50

Foreword
Mary Esther Huerta, PhD

Every newborn child enters the world with the "at promise" aspirations assigned by the welcoming caretakers and family members. Each newborn also adds to the range of diversity readily apparent among young children when considering unique physical features, personalities, varying uses of executive functions that influence levels of awareness, among other important attributes. In addition, the young child's attributes will be framed by the particular sociocultural practices of the home that also co-exist with unpredictable real world that affects daily life.

The continuous shifting contexts of home, community, and world events that envelope the life of every child will differentiate how young children think, speak, play, solve problems, and learn. Ultimately, while each child is left to navigate and manage shifting social contexts to meet their needs and intentions, the varying level of support each receives influences opportunities to access and benefit from the institutions, resources, and materials available within their particular society. Equitable access of resources and materials depends largely on the societal values and beliefs of the dominant majority group.

Further, in western societies each stage of development of the young child will be evaluated using metrics sustained by research and practice. These metrics assess cognitive, socio-emotional, sociocultural, linguistic, and physical development, and many become benchmarks in early childhood development. Research has sustained these benchmarks by studies that prioritize young children from families belonging to the dominant social group of society.

When the literature demonstrates how the socioeconomic and the sociocultural practices of a child's family parallel those of the dominant majority, reported findings establish child development norms, demonstrating also how the young child-member of the dominant majority social group is "at promise" of seamlessly benefiting from available institutions, resources, and materials of the society. When the research findings become developmental benchmarks, they guide the expectations of caretakers, pediatricians, educators, and other social institutional systems.

Moreover, these benchmarks are perpetuated when they are applied as overarching governing educational policies that classify young children as either being "at risk" of academic failure or being "at promise" of obtaining academic achievement upon entering school. As educational standards, these binary classifications have historically measured differentiated levels of achievements between young children from culturally and linguistically diverse backgrounds and young children-members of the dominant majority group. As these standards are integrated with school culture and instructional practices, the classifications assigned to each child are reinforced, remaining rigid throughout the schooling journey.

The culture of schooling and the instructional practices, normed for young children who belong to dominant majority, highlight the timeliness of the chapters included in this volume. Each chapter offers educational approaches that amplify equity in accessing appropriate instruction for young children from culturally and linguistically diverse backgrounds. The studies explored relevant instruction targeting typically developing young children from culturally and linguistically diverse backgrounds as well as instruction for young children who additionally need the support of special education programs.

In particular, the third chapter unifies the collection by describing modes of strengthening home to school partnerships in a teacher preparation program. The goal of these partnerships is to enhance instruction by engaging parents through meaningful communication that also establishes robust relationships. It is through dialogic communication with parents that each young child's identity can be leveraged to nurture the whole child, in particular those who are bicultural and multilingual.

Today, early childhood education exists within a global society, requiring that issues of diversity exist vibrantly at the core of all teaching and learning experiences. Changes toward enhancing access and equity in educational opportunities begin with teachers and the pedagogy that they offer. In combination, the studies in this volume offer relevant perspectives and instructional practices that sustain the cognitive, cultural and linguistic, and socio-emotional development of young children as global citizens. In this vein, the authors have situated diversity at the core of early childhood education, providing significant pedagogy that enables young children to enhance self-representation competencies.

As children develop agency and voice to express their purposes, needs, and intentions, they widen thinking and learning pathways that challenge existing social boundaries to secure their well-being as members of their community, their nation, and their global society.

Introduction
Mari Riojas-Cortez

As I write this introduction there are protests happening all over the United States because of the killing of George Floyd. This happens as the country tries to live with a deadly virus that unfortunately targets communities of color. There is much disagreement about how and if protests should occur while members of communities of color continue to die of complications from COVID-19. For many families it is unfathomable to think how their children are targeted because of the color of their skin. Children are listening and watching and they often wonder if such brutalities will happen to them. The truth is that such physical brutalities may not happen in the classroom but emotional brutalities will occur unless change occurs.

A change in disposition and views toward children and families of color is highly needed. Being color blind is not an option. Families of color face oppression in their daily lives from working low-wage jobs to lack of health care and low-quality child care. Such oppression leads to other health problems including mental health and even substance abuse which is often used as a stereotype for many people of color. Persistent poverty is seen across the United States but is heavily prevalent in the southern states. Undocumented families live in fear of being deported although they contribute to the economy. Access to high-quality early childhood programs is also a struggle for families of color. The list of oppression unfortunately continues housing, food insecurity, job opportunities, education, and so on.

Very often the hurdles of society are too much for educators but without their understanding such hurdles will continue. Preservice teachers must know and understand the history, injustices, and struggles that communities of color endure. In order to increase that understanding, faculty who teach in teacher preparation programs must take the lead and discover ways to best reach preservice teachers. This book presents examples of faculty taking the lead to help preservice teachers understand the social injustices in aspects of early childhood education. This move can lead to highly qualified early childhood teachers.

Quality-early childhood programs begin with highly qualified teachers. However, usually the notion of what classifies a high-quality teacher often focuses on teaching credentials and salaries. Although the two are important it is just as important that teachers are knowledgeable of culturally responsive practices (Young et al., 2018). In short, it is not enough to be prepared and to be well paid, it is extremely important that teachers practice culturally responsive teaching that promotes the success of all children but in particular and those that are most vulnerable, children of color. In addition, it is just as important to provide the least restrictive environment for children with special needs which is part of inclusive responsive teaching.

Diversifying pedagogy means that preservice teachers know cultural and inclusive responsive approaches for marginalized children. For instance, knowing appropriate early literacy practices that are culturally appropriate for dual language learners (DLLs) can provide higher opportunities for children who are immigrants or who speak another language than English at home. Being aware and knowing the implementation of practice and policy can help dual language learners in the development of not only bilingualism but also biliteracy. Inclusive practices are essential for the success of children who have special needs. Engaging with parents means developing partnerships that serve as a strong foundation for children's learning.

The teaching of race has to be taught in teacher preparation programs. Faculty must look for ways to eradicate racist perceptions. Such perceptions may include negative views of how people live, the way they speak or the language they speak, child rearing practices, education, housing, and more. Understanding and identifying own biases is a start. Next step includes the revising goals and objectives of the teacher preparation program to show how issues of race are covered. It is not a matter of integration but it is a matter of using a different lens. Change in society can be brought about through the education of teachers and that is diversifying pedagogy.

Chapter 1

Perceptions and Misconceptions

How Best to Prepare Early Childhood Teachers to Work with Dual Language Learners

Cristina Gillanders and Marlene Zepeda

People of the world are on the move. More than ever before, the world population is migrating from the place where they were born (IOM, 2019) to a new country. Immigration is nearing the historic record at 13.4% of the U.S. population (Pew Research Center, 2019). Immigrants may bring along their loved ones or create new families in their host country. They also bring their language and cultural practices. In an increasingly interconnected and interdependent world, speaking more than one language in a pluralistic society can be a functional asset.

Since its inception, the United States has benefited enormously from the contributions of immigrants. The majority of bilingual children in the United States are the children of immigrants, but bilingualism is also found among the U.S.-born population. For example, 72% of U.S.-born Latinos ages 18–33 years or younger speak both Spanish and English (Patten, 2016). Yet, despite their significant contribution to society, individuals who have the potential to speak another language and come from certain groups (e.g., of color and lower socioeconomic status) are viewed as a problem to overcome.

In the context of this chapter, the terms "dual language learner" (DLL) and "bilingual" will refer to children who are younger than five and are learning two or more languages simultaneously from birth or once they begin to attend an early childhood program. Another term to use with this population is "emergent bilingual" as many children in the United States grow up in a home where two languages are spoken (García et al., 2008). "Emergent bilinguals" in early childhood live in a context where they hear the home language at home and acquire English at early childhood centers or through other family members such as siblings, cousins, and extended family that may care for them.

The growing diversity in the United States, including children whose home language is not English, presents challenges for educator preparation. One reason for the view of bilingual children as a "problem" or "challenge" is that few teachers have had the preparation and professional development to work with bilingual children. More than ten years ago, only a small percentage (10.8%) of teacher preparation programs at the BA level required a dedicated course and/or integration of linguistic diversity content in coursework (Lim et al., 2009).

Although we are hopeful that this situation has changed in recent years, there is no evidence that a significant number of teacher preparation programs offer courses with a focus in bilingual children. A more recent study on state teacher certification standards revealed that states have, at best, very minimal standards for preparation to work with bilingual children, and many have no requirements at all (Samson & Collins, 2012). In general, teacher preparation programs have not kept up with the demographic changes of the country.

This chapter discusses how preparing teachers to work with young DLLs or bilingual children is an opportunity to convey to both new and experienced teachers that nurturing the potential of these children is their responsibility, even when the educational system views them as a conundrum. Consequently, in this chapter, we first discuss the importance of preparing teachers to promote bilingual children's learning and development, then describe the competencies that early childhood educators should have to work with bilingual children, and finally present promising practices to teach these competencies.

EARLY CHILDHOOD TEACHER PREPARATION IN AN ERA OF GREAT DEMOGRAPHIC CHANGE

Given the changing demographic landscape, early childhood educators are increasingly called upon to serve children from diverse language and cultural backgrounds. The diversity of our child population presents challenges to our understanding of how children grow and develop and has implications for both the content and recommended pedagogical practice promoted in early educator education and preparation. In order to adequately prepare educators serving young children, our central task is twofold.

First, we must understand the universal properties of child growth and development that are applicable to all children regardless of cultural and linguistic background. Second and most importantly, we must recognize the distinct needs of children whose culture and language are different from the mainstream (NAEYC, 2019a). The field is increasingly recognizing that child development is a cultural process (Rogoff, 2003), and has moved from viewing differences as deficits to viewing them as beneficial assets that merit support.

The National Association for the Education of Young Children (NAEYC, 2019a) has articulated guidance to assist early educators in their nurturance and pedagogical practice with young children. While reaffirming their previous focus on sensitive and appropriate caregiving, intentional teaching, accurate assessment and the importance of family engagement, the revised statement on Developmentally Appropriate Practice (DAP) explicitly broadens its focus by emphasizing aspects of the environment in which a child resides.

Specifically, the cultural and linguistic context in which a child develops provides a backdrop that early educators must accommodate and consider. DAP acknowledges that the language development and the trajectory of a bilingual child is different from that of a monolingual and that these differences should be perceived as strengths rather than deficits.

Additionally, the concept of "windows and mirrors" in pedagogical practice (Bishop, 1990) deserves attention for DLLs. The idea here is that the learning environment (e.g., materials and activities) should mirror or reflect the children's identities, including their families and neighborhoods, while at the same time providing windows or avenues to access new experiences and opportunities. This concept speaks to how the early learning environment can preserve a child's sense of self while simultaneously serving as a bridge between different cultures and languages.

It is widely acknowledged that access to high-quality early education is associated with positive academic and social outcomes for young children (Pre-kindergarten Task Force, 2017). For DLLs, in particular, the evidence is clear that participation in high-quality early care is beneficial (Burchinal, 2018). As many DLLs come from immigrant families in low-income circumstances, accessibility to high-quality early care and education has been shown to be limited (Gelatt et al., 2014). Since every child has the right to equitable learning opportunities, all educators have the ethical obligation to promote equity in their practice (NAEYC, 2019b). What does this mean for addressing the needs of young DLLs?

DLLs need to learn both a new language and have access to the content of learning experiences in a language they may not know or understand; thus, it is only fair that adjustments and accommodations in teaching and learning are made so that they can fully participate in their educational experience. Issues of diversity and inclusiveness reflective of an equitable learning environment are salient when working with all children, but because DLLs come from varied language and cultural backgrounds, these issues become magnified and require particular attention.

WHAT SHOULD EARLY EDUCATORS KNOW

The term "educator competencies" refers to the knowledge, skills, and dispositions necessary to work effectively with children and families. Explicit competencies provide a framework for performance expectations of educators and can assist in the development of preservice and in-service education and training. There have been a number of efforts to synthesize and describe educator competencies that optimize the development of young DLLs (Oliva-Olson et al., 2017; Lopez et al., 2012; Zepeda et al., 2011).

A recent review of existing state learning and development standards for young DLLs by Espinosa and Calderon (2015) suggests a growing awareness of the importance of describing the specific characteristics of the development of young DLLs for educators. These authors point out the need for state standards to include specific teacher qualifications that will prepare them to address DLLs' distinct needs.

Reviewing the literature, Zepeda et al. (2011) identified competency areas that merit attention for educator knowledge and skill development when working with young DLLs. These areas include:

- Understanding language development,
- Understanding the relationship between language and culture,
- Developing skills and abilities to effectively teach DLLs,
- Developing abilities to use assessment in meaningful ways with DLLs,
- Developing a sense of professionalism, and
- Understanding how to work with families.

These competencies are not only for early educators who have a high number of bilingual children in their classroom—it is very likely that in the course of their professional careers, all early educators will teach children from bilingual environments.

The National Academy of Sciences synthesis report on bilingual children and youth concludes that the early years are optimal for learning two or more languages and that there are significant linguistic and cognitive advantages associated with bilingualism (NASEM, 2017). In addition, the NASEM report notes that strong levels of home language and English are needed for future academic success and, notably, that home language loss can negatively affect a child's positive relationship with their families and culture of origin. In order to appropriately serve young DLLs, early educators need to understand their typical development and school readiness, what external influences affect their learning, and what teaching practices are most effective for them (Espinosa & Zepeda, 2019).

"Culturally responsive" teaching is an often-discussed over-riding competency. Gay (2010) defines culturally responsive teaching as possessing knowledge about diverse children including understanding their previous experiences, how they perceive the world, and their approaches to learning. The concept of linguistically responsive teaching intersects with culturally responsive teaching, but its focus is on instructional methods related to optimal language learning in DLLs.

Paris (2012) has extended the concept of culturally responsive teaching to culturally sustaining pedagogy, which refers to ways of teaching that are "more than responsive of or relevant to the cultural experiences and practices of young people—it requires that they support young people in sustaining the cultural and linguistic competence of their communities while simultaneously offering access to dominant cultural competence" (Paris, 2012, p. 95).

AREAS OF KNOWLEDGE AND UNDERSTANDING

What are the salient areas of knowledge and understanding that ECE educators need in order to effectively serve young children whose home language is not English? The following discussion highlights important background knowledge that clarifies why supporting a child's home language and culture will promote their overall learning and facilitate their academic performance. Specific instructional approaches supporting language and literacy development are outlined.

Language development. Knowledge of how first and second languages develop will be of benefit to the early educator serving young DLLs because it provides the basis for implementing specialized pedagogical practice. In order to effectively interact with DLL children and families, it is important that educators understand the process of general language development. For example, what are the normative expectations for language production and complexity of speech across the early years for all children regardless of their primary language? The universal aspects of language development provide the basis for understanding how a second language interacts with and builds on a first language.

Although DLLs follow a similar general language trajectory to monolingual children, their development will demonstrate unique characteristics as a function of learning two languages. These include code-mixing, smaller vocabularies in each language (Hammer et al., 2014) and differences in the emergence of linguistic elements. More recently, researchers have found that bilinguals often access different linguistic features of the languages they speak in order to maximize communication, a practice referred to as translanguaging (García, 2009).

In addition, in order for early educators to work effectively with young DLLs it is important that they possess a general understanding of the process of simultaneous and sequential bilingualism; that is, exposure to two languages at the same time versus substantial exposure to one language prior to learning a second language. The quantity and quality of a DLL child's early language exposure in their different languages present educators with the challenge of identifying the process of language development, which may vary in each of the child's languages, and adjusting their pedagogy accordingly.

An important developmental process connected to language development for young DLLs is how their brains develop differently from monolingual brains. There is a growing body of research demonstrating that bilingual infants process information differently than monolingual children, leading to increased brain activity (Conboy, 2013). This distinction in information processing fosters enhanced attention to visual processing (Sebastian-Galles et al., 2011) and sound cues during speech processing (Kovacs & Mehler, 2009), as well as greater advantage in executive control tasks (Poulin-Dubois et al., 2011).

Research suggests that because bilinguals must adjust their perceptual attention between two languages, they are, by necessity, more flexible learners. This research points to the cognitive advantage that bilingualism holds for young DLLs (Bialystok, 2011). Understanding the bilingual brain can help dispel the misconception that bilingualism is a source of confusion for the young child.

Relationship between language and culture. Language and culture are completely interwoven and, taken together, form the basis for a child's socialization and identity development (Schieffelin & Ochs, 1986). Language acquisition plays a central role in "becoming a person" (Shatz, 1994, p.7) and a member of a particular cultural group through the transmission of cultural values (Halle et al., 2014). Not only are children socialized through the use of language, they are also socialized about how to use the language.

For example, such issues as who initiates conversation, what physical distance should there be between speakers, and how cultural hierarchical patterns of authority influence communicative turn taking are modeled for children by family members through daily interaction. Young DLLs participating in out of home care and education settings may be exposed to conflicting socialization practices, expressed through both the behavior and language of educators. Continuity or discontinuity in the languages between settings can potentially influence a child's well-being, "including the development of self-concept, positive social adjustment and identity" (Halle et al., 2014, p. 737).

A child's primary language is their means of accessing information about their culture and may be linked to a positive socio-emotional trajectory (Halle et al., 2014). However, exposure to a new language and culture may result in a child losing their primary language (Guiberson et al., 2006). This, in turn, may have a negative effect on communication in the family, with the associated loss of trust and feelings of parental control (Tannenbaum & Berkovich, 2005), in addition to the loss of the benefits brought by bilingualism. Thus, it is important that educators not only value the primary language but also incorporate it within the existing curricular parameters of their programs.

Instructional approaches associated with positive academic outcome. A number of reviews have identified appropriate teaching strategies when working with young DLLs (Castro et al., 2011; Espinosa, 2015). However, teaching approaches will vary based on a program's specific curricular model and goals and objectives for first and second language development. There is a general consensus regarding instructional strategies and enhancements that have been linked to improved achievement of DLLs in early education settings (NASEM, 2017; Espinosa & Zepeda, 2019). The majority of these strategies focus on language and literacy development.

Use of the home language. Because the use of the home language while the child acquires English is associated with higher rates of English proficiency (Castro et al., 2011), early educators who intentionally use the home language across content areas will assist DLLs in the development of their conceptual knowledge. In addition, if DLLs are given opportunities to develop listening, speaking, writing, and reading skills in both their languages, over time they will demonstrate higher levels of academic achievement in elementary school (Valentino & Reardon, 2015). Several studies have also found that using children's home language leads to higher social, cognitive, and academic achievement levels for bilingual learners (e.g., Burchinal et al., 2012).

Explicit vocabulary instruction. Providing DLLs with the definitions of specific vocabulary words in both their home language and English and exposing them to print in a variety of contexts (e.g., storybook reading, daily schedules, labels on objects) will assist in comprehension and oral language skills. Meaningful repetition of vocabulary across different activities will expand their understanding of word meaning (Gillanders et al., 2014).

Intentional oral language development and literacy. As strong oral language skills are associated with such future literacy capabilities as narrative and discourse production and reading comprehension (Shanahan & Lonigan, 2010), young children need ample purposeful opportunities for listening and speaking to experiment in each language. For DLLs, the need to practice speaking is greater, as they must process verbal information using two different sound systems and grammatical patterns.

According to the NASEM report (2017), oral language development includes a focus on phonological awareness, vocabulary development, listening comprehension skills, speaking and narrative skills, and interaction with speakers proficient in the second language, particularly adults who provide corrective feedback during verbal interactions. Furthermore, teachers should understand how they can promote biliteracy in young DLLs. They can, for example, promote enjoyment of reading by exposing children to texts in both English and their home language (Espinosa, 2015). Educators can provide opportunities for children to write in different languages and to become aware of the commonalities and differences among languages (Gillanders & Soltero-González, 2019).

Explicit bridging between the home language and English. The provision of pictures and visual cues or physical gestures that convey meaning will help children comprehend and retain academic content. Although these approaches are good practice for all young children, they are especially needed for children who do not understand English and cannot be expected to rely solely on oral language input. This strategy can enhance children's comprehension and participation in the classroom (Gillanders et al., 2014).

Opportunities to participate in small groups. DLLs, like all young children, need individual attention. However, because DLLs are learning a new language, they benefit from additional practice time to reinforce both comprehension and production of language. During small group time, more hands-on and interactive activities can be afforded that will deepen their understanding. Also, teachers can be more intentional in the scaffolding of learning experiences and can more closely monitor children's learning (Landry et al., 2019).

Opportunities to interact with peers. Recent research demonstrates the important role that peers play in language development for DLLs (Sawyer et al., 2018). During informal peer interaction, DLLs have the opportunity to practice their budding language skills without feeling adult pressure. Structuring early learning environments that promote informal peer interaction provides additional learning time.

Incorporate elements of the children's home culture. Evidence suggests that creating a supportive environment reflective of a child's language and culture will help to engage the child and support a positive learning climate (Howes, 2010). Incorporating families' "funds of knowledge" provides opportunities for children to use language, literacy, and mathematics in authentic and meaningful ways (Riojas-Cortez, 2001).

Purposeful Assessment. Because DLLs' language knowledge is divided between each of their languages, they tend to demonstrate slower rates of development in each language when compared to monolingual children (Bialystok & Feng, 2011). Yet, Garcia et al. (2016) show this repertoire as a continuum that occurs across two languages that is neither segmented nor divided. Thus, emergent bilinguals have a high cognitive ability who can flexibly retrieve from linguistic repertoire that includes two linguistic systems to align thought and language with a particular context.

Thus, in order to obtain a fair and appropriate (equitable) measure of the knowledge and skills of DLLS, assessment should be conducted in both languages (Espinosa, 2010). Although there are a limited number of valid and reliable assessments developed for young children learning two languages (Barrueco et al., 2012), there is a process that educators can follow to ensure they are appropriately measuring children's development for individualizing and enhancing their educational experiences (see Espinosa & Gutierrez-Clellan, 2013).

Early educators need to be skilled observers with knowledge of both a DLL's culture and how second language development occurs. As the family is the educator's best informant about their child's development, it is important to involve them in the assessment process (Espinosa & McClellan, 2013). In addition, educators need to understand the limitations of current assessment and interpret assessment results accordingly.

Professionalism and advocacy. One of the first steps in learning about DLLs is for educators to examine their own beliefs and assumptions about how these young children develop and learn (Gay, 2010). Educator competency with DLLs is affected by their dispositions to operationalize linguistically and culturally appropriate practice within the broader societal context in which their services are rendered. In the development of differentiated teacher competencies for serving young DLLs (Lopez et al., 2012), Atencio (cited in Lopez et al., 2012) articulated four competency areas reflective of educators' attitudes for working with DLLs. They are:

1. Establish an ongoing commitment to building one's competency and knowledge level about teaching young DLLs.
2. Maintain a commitment to develop cultural responsiveness in the teaching of children from diverse linguistic and cultural backgrounds.
3. Develop and sustain a consciousness of the broader social realities confronting DLL populations while maintaining a commitment to care for, support, and nurture young learners and their families in their natural linguistic and cultural realities and advocate for their rights as citizens.
4. Develop and sustain a high tolerance for ambiguity, maintain an ability to live within and negotiate contradictions in pedagogy, and resolve ethical and policy dilemmas while maintaining a resilient attitude toward social and economic challenges surrounding DLL children, their families, and themselves as DLL educators.

These dispositions describe an educator who is open to cultural pluralism and willing to advocate for what is in the best interest of young DLLs and their families with all its attendant complexity.

Home-School Partnerships. The developing child learns about their culture through their interactions with their parents and other family members. Differences in goals underlying caregiving practices may become a source of confusion for families and children (Shrivers et al., 2011). One of the best ways to prevent potential cultural misunderstandings is by initiating and maintaining a dialogue with parents and other family members.

Through dialogue with families about their childrearing beliefs, practices, and expectations, educators can integrate culturally and linguistically responsive practices into their own program's goals and objectives. Educators who acknowledge that families possess "funds of knowledge" reflective of their own culturally derived skills and competencies (Moll et al., 1992) and utilize that knowledge in their practice can help reduce incongruity for the young child.

Although family engagement is a shared responsibility between families and educators (Weiss et al., 2014), the onus to initiate contact and provide opportunities for parents to engage with educators should begin with educators themselves. As many DLLs come from immigrant families where little English is spoken in the home and which may be unfamiliar with the operation of educational and social services, they are unlikely to take the first step in establishing educator-family partnerships. Educators need to develop and incorporate procedures and processes for routine communication with families (NAEYC, 2010a).

PROMISING PRACTICES IN THE PREPARATION OF EARLY CHILDHOOD TEACHERS

Working with Dual Language Learners

As we reviewed the existing literature on the preparation of early childhood teachers to work with bilingual children, we found that most of the examples come from teacher preparation at the K-12 level. Fewer examples can be found in the field of early childhood education. It is only recently that early childhood teacher preparation programs have focused on preparing educators to work with young bilingual children.

Since much of the teacher preparation in the field of early childhood happens at the in-service level, we have included some examples of studies examining professional development interventions geared to developing competencies in early childhood educators to work with bilingual children. We have also reviewed a few examples of teacher preparation in higher education settings that illustrate important aspects of early childhood teacher preparation. The chosen studies describe competencies and dispositions necessary for early educators to work with bilingual children and their families.

Professional Development Interventions

Use of English and home language. In the field of education, the use of languages other than English in the classroom has been a controversial topic for many years. However, many studies have revealed that using the language children listen to and speak at home is important for their development and learning and their potential to become bilinguals (NASEM, 2017). Given the importance of using both English and the home language in the classroom, a few studies have examined the effects of professional development interventions on the ability of teachers to include both languages in their everyday interactions with children.

Castro et al. (2017) conducted an experimental study to assess the efficacy of the *Nuestros Niños* School Readiness (NNSR) Professional Development Program, a 2-year program that included an integrative approach to teacher professional development to promote language, literacy, and social-emotional development, and mathematics learning in pre-kindergarten Spanish-English DLLs. Teachers in the *Nuestros Niños* program received two summer institutes on the language and literacy development of DLLs, coaching/consultation every other week for 2 years, and twice a month opportunities to discuss strategies to promote language in professional learning communities in the first year and once a month during the second.

Castro and colleagues found that more Spanish was spoken by teachers in the treatment group in their interactions with DLL children, and this effect increased from year 1 to year 2 of their participation in the program. As expected, this result was particularly evident in classrooms in which the lead and assistant teachers were bilingual and had participated in the intervention for 2 years. Although this might be obvious, it is also true that in many classrooms in which there was a bilingual adult, the home language was seldom used. In a follow-up study conducted by Franco et al. (2019), the researchers found that even in classrooms with a bilingual adult, and where the majority of children spoke Spanish, few linguistic interactions happened in Spanish. The findings from these two studies suggest that even though having bilingual adults in the classroom may increase the likelihood that the home language is used, teachers need preparation in strategic use of the home language, especially in classrooms in which a bilingual approach has not been adopted. The study also revealed that teachers' concern for children's school readiness for English-only kindergarten might influence their decisions about using the children's home language.

Spies et al. (2017) also found that teachers' previous beliefs influence the effects of a professional development. In their study, they examined the influence of a professional development on the instructional practices and beliefs regarding bilingualism in a group of early childhood lead teachers and aides. The professional development consisted of six three-hour sessions that included topics such as language and literacy development in DLLs, second language acquisition, classroom materials and environments, parent engagement and assessment. All sessions included opportunities for participants to implement some of the practices discussed during the professional development.

Using a pre- and post-survey, study findings indicated that participants made changes in their beliefs regarding the role of the home language, instructional practices, and the role of the family. In post-professional development focus groups, participants expressed that empathy was an important ability that influenced their decisions in the classroom with regards to DLLs. Furthermore, preparing children for kindergarten and accountability testing was also a motivator to implement teaching strategies stressing English. Participants in the study reported lack of materials and language proficiency as significant limitations. The researchers concluded that these beliefs mediated teachers' behaviors as a result of their participation in the professional development.

Overall, these studies indicate that teachers need some guidance on how to use the home language strategically in the classroom and that professional development can dispel some of the misconceptions they might have about bilingualism. They also reveal that opportunities for professional development need to explicitly make connections between theory and practice with opportunities for practice in on-the-job settings, immediate feedback after the rehearsal of skills, as well as collective participation and structures for staff collaboration (Zaslow et al., 2010).

Working with families and communities. In a prekindergarten-university partnership, Hardin et al. (2010) designed a professional development program aimed at assisting early childhood teachers and teacher assistants in implementing culturally and linguistically relevant practices in classrooms with a large percentage of DLLs and immigrant children. The professional development included three "interactive training sessions" which included topics such as:

1. Strategies for identifying sociocultural practices,
2. Teaching strategies to support second language acquisition, and
3. Effective approaches for promoting home, school, and community partnerships.

The program also included coaching visits in which doctoral students supported teachers in the implementation of effective strategies. Participants indicated high satisfaction with both the interactive sessions and the coaching. Teaching staff demonstrated more effort to communicate with families.

Evident were also changes in the arrangement of the physical environment, materials, and resources reflective of children's sociocultural experiences.

A key aspect of implementing culturally sustaining pedagogy is to uncover the wealth of sociocultural practices children participate in at home and translate them into the classroom. As such, teachers need to be well-versed about the families and communities' funds of knowledge. A particularly well-suited vehicle for teachers to learn about families are home visits.

In a professional development program focused on developmentally and culturally responsive teaching, Whyte and Karabon (2016) examined teachers' home visits to learn more about the children's funds of knowledge. The findings indicate that teachers reproduced the power relations that are common in traditional parent involvement. Teachers had preconceived notions of the role of families in their children's education, and their questions and connections with the families reflected these notions. Through opportunities for reflection and dialogue, the boundaries between teacher's role and that of the families began to blur and true interest in learning about the families' strengths and resources began to emerge.

The examples provided illustrate that intentional efforts are needed in teacher education to prepare early educators to work within culturally sustaining pedagogy. Preparation should include supporting early educators in their efforts to learn from families and incorporate sociocultural practices in the classroom in a way that is culturally sustaining. Within these efforts, teacher educators need to consider that educators bring with them preconceived notions of power structures between teachers and families and that these need to be explicitly addressed through opportunities for dialogue and reflection on their own practice.

TEACHER PREPARATION IN HIGHER EDUCATION

Few examples exist in the literature of higher education programs emphasizing working with DLLs. Given the "demographic imperative" (Achinstein et al., 2010) of preparing early educators to work with DLLs, Mueller and File (2015) proposed a revisioning process of their early childhood teacher education program to prepare students to be "well prepared to engage with a variety of strengths, learning needs, personalities, cultural assets, language needs and developmental attributes evident in any group of young children with whom they would work" (Mueller & File, 2015, p. 182).

Realizing the need to "keep up with the times," the faculty set up goals and made programmatic changes in order to reach this goal. Among their programmatic changes, they required coursework in linguistic and language acquisition, integration of content related to DLLs in courses related to

STEM and literacy, field experiences with DLLs. In collaboration with the English as a Second Language Department (ESL), they also designed an add-on on ESL and/or bilingual education certification.

Programmatic revisions require being well-versed about working with DLLs to integrate learning opportunities in coursework through the necessary competencies. In an effort to prepare faculty, McCrary et al. (2011) report on an early childhood education faculty's effort to learn more about working with DLLs. Different strategies were used including inviting experts at faculty colloquiums, engaging in book studies, attending conferences, and conducting classroom visits. Moreover, faculty identified a series of competencies they wanted their students to gain as a result of the program and revised their courses to infuse learning opportunities that addressed these competencies. At the end of the program, faculty and students reported increased knowledge about teaching DLLs.

Another approach is to collaborate with faculty experienced in culturally and linguistically diverse preservice teacher education. Baecher (a TESOL teacher educator) and Jewkes (an ECE teacher educator) (2014) worked collaboratively to create an experience for early childhood education and TESOL teacher candidates in which both groups analyzed a set of videos of teaching a young group of DLLs. Findings showed the benefit of a collaborative inquiry between students and faculty, the similarities and differences between the fields of ECE and TESOL, and the need to provide more experiences in early childhood to TESOL students with emphasis on the education of DLLs to ECE students.

Ironically, in this review of literature we have found that professional development independent of the higher education setting seems to be more flexible and creative than courses in university settings. It is possible that, given the curricular change process in universities, innovation might be limited. Because coursework must be in alignment with a state's certification standards for authorization and accreditation, the state's overall licensing standards are highly influential in determining a program's coursework. This may limit an institution of higher education's perceived need to expand and/or integrate content applicable to DLLs.

Diversity in the Early Childhood Educators' Population

Although most teachers who serve DLLs are monolingual English speakers (NASEM, 2017), it is important to consider the broad variability in teacher characteristics relative to their particular language and cultural orientation as well as their years of experience working with DLLs. It is to be expected that skills and abilities will also vary based on educator backgrounds. Instructional competencies focused on the DLL population must include approaches for educators who do not know the child's home language. All educators, regardless of their language and cultural backgrounds, can successfully serve young DLLs.

Lopez et al. (2012) present teacher competencies focused on language and literacy and socio-emotional development presents a matrix of instructional competencies based on varying language abilities and cultural knowledge. These competencies are based on whether the educator speaks and/or is literate in the target language of the child, and how knowledgeable they are of the target child's culture. The matrix further differentiates early educators by years of experience serving DLLs (e.g., beginning, developing, and advanced). This matrix demonstrates that the acquisition of pedagogical competence is a developmental process for the educators themselves and must be adjusted based on their personal characteristics. See Figure 1.1 for an example.

Programs in early childhood education should also make efforts to recruit individuals who are bilingual and have similar backgrounds to the children they teach. Since many of these teacher candidates of color are non-traditional students, higher education programs should consider the structural barriers these students confront. Efforts should be made to ensure access to

	Monolingual		Bilingual		Biliterate	
	Monocultural	**Bicultural**	**Monocultural**	**Bicultural**	**Monocultural**	**Bicultural**
DEVELOPING	Skills: • Demonstrates a growing understanding of language milestones and processes in the first language and English. • Is able to identify the different stages of second language development in individual DLL children. • Demonstrates growing abilities to verbally stimulate conversation with DLL children using English. • In interactions with children and families, shows a growing awareness of how culture influences communication (e.g., eye contact, use of proper names, etc.).	Skills: • Demonstrates a growing understanding of language milestones and processes in the first language and English. • Is able to identify the different stages of second language development in individual DLL children. • Demonstrates growing abilities to verbally stimulate conversation with DLLs using English. • In interactions with children and families, shows growing familiarity with how culture influences communication (e.g., eye contact, use of proper names, etc.).	Skills: • Demonstrates a growing understanding of language milestones and processes in the first language and English. • Is able to identify the different stages of second language development in individual DLL children. • Uses both languages in interactions with children.	Skills: • Demonstrates a growing understanding of language milestones and processes in the first language and English. • Is able to identify the different stages of second language development in individual DLL children. • Uses both languages in interactions with children. • In interactions with children and families, shows growing familiarity with how culture influences communication (e.g., eye contact, use of proper names, etc.).	Skills: • Demonstrates a growing understanding of language milestones and processes in the first language and English. • Is able to identify the different stages of second language development in individual DLL children. • Uses both languages while interacting with children. • Utilizes written information in the first language to assist instruction.	Skills: • Demonstrates a growing understanding of language milestones and processes in the first language and English. • Is able to identify the different stages of second language development in individual DLL children. • Uses both languages while interacting with children. • Utilizes written information in the first language to assist instruction. • In interactions with children and families, shows growing familiarity with how culture influences communication (e.g., eye contact, use of proper names, etc.).
	Indicators: • Uses more of the teaching strategies described for the beginning teacher. • Begins to match a child's stage of second language acquisition with a specific teaching strategy (e.g., telegraphic speech and interactive games such as Simon Says). • Accepts language mixing as normal in DLL development. • Repeats and expands what child has said. • Observes parent and child behavior during arrival and departure to determine appropriate expectations for communication.	Indicators: • Accepts children's culturally defined social behavior (e.g., hugging, bowing, kissing). • Uses culturally appropriate behavior during greeting and departing. • Demonstrates growing abilities to engage DLL children in sustained conversation using English.	Indicators: • Uses running narrative to describe what a child is doing (e.g., you're painting big and little circles with different colors, red, yellow, green). • Uses puppets and other visuals to promote expressive language in either language. • Asks another staff member to explain particular cultural differences that they notice (e.g., respect for the teacher's role requires that parents always appear to be in agreement). • Plays "I spy" in the first language and English within the classroom and outdoors to stimulate vocabulary acquisition.	Indicators: • Engages in extended conversations in the child's first language using rich vocabulary and complex sentences. • Explains idioms in English to children in their first language or provides them with comparable idioms in their first language (e.g., "raining cats and dogs / a cántaros, maybe / a lo mejor"). • Understands and can use cultural sayings to convey meaning/idea indirectly (e.g., "A child with one chopstick goes hungry").	Indicators: • Seeks out and uses written information to expand knowledge about specific vocabulary and concepts in the first language that can be used in teaching (e.g., reviews neighborhood newspaper). • Uses dialogic reading strategies to expand vocabulary and encourage comprehension in first language and English. • Takes dictation from children in first language and English.	Indicators: • Uses the first language to expand a DLL child's verbalization by asking open-ended questions to encourage extended conversations. • Uses photos of neighborhood stores and businesses with first language signs/labels and shows them to the children to discuss what happens in that context (e.g., laundry mat).

Figure 1.1 Matrix of Pedagogical Competence of Early Educators Working with DLLs.
Source: Provided by author.

state tests, financial support, academic writing and mathematical skills, and flexible scheduling (Gillanders et al., 2020).

CONCLUSIONS AND RECOMMENDATIONS FOR TEACHER PREPARATION

As the child population grows more diverse, it is incumbent upon teacher preparation programs to develop curricula and practicum that provide future educators with the necessary knowledge, skills, and dispositions to optimize the development of their students. It is also important for teacher preparation programs to understand that addressing the needs of diverse children means confronting long-standing social inequities that have deleterious effects for the optimal development of children (NAEYC, 2019).

In our experience working with early childhood educators, we have learned that developing the necessary knowledge, skills, and dispositions takes time, so no single course will address all the competencies described here. Early childhood teacher preparation programs should also consider embedding content related to DLLs in multiple courses, especially those that make explicit connections with practice and provide opportunities for interaction with families, reflection, and dialogue. This chapter provides guidance for teacher educators about teacher behaviors and abilities that advance the development of young DLLs.

Examples from Practice

In this section, we have included a few examples of assignments that could be incorporated in different courses to address the knowledge, skills, and dispositions described in this chapter.

1.
    a) Read Suárez-Orozco, C., Yoshikawa, H., & Tseng, V. (2015). Intersecting inequalities: Research to reduce inequality for immigrant-origin children and youth. *William T. Grant Foundation.* Retrieved from: http://wtgrantfoundation.org/library/uploads/2015/09/Intersecting-Inequalities-Research-to-Reduce-Inequality-for-Immigrant-Origin-Children-and-Youth.pdf
    b) Find one blog, website, video, interview, news article, and so on that expands, supports, or refutes the claims described in the Suarez-Orozco et al. report and illustrates the media coverage of immigrant families and their children.

    c) Bring the media coverage example and be prepared to present it to the class.
2.
    a) Read Espinosa, L. M. (2013). *PreK-3rd: Challenging common myths about dual language learners: An update to the Seminal 2008 report.* New York, NY: Foundation for Child Development. Retrieved from: https://www.fcd-us.org/assets/2016/04/Challenging-Common-Myths-Update.pdf
    b) Find a co-worker, parent, family member, or friend and ask if they agree or disagree with the myths described in the Espinosa (2013) report.
    c) Make sure you ask their reasons for agreeing or disagreeing with these statements. Take notes and bring to class. Discuss the findings of your interview in light of the Espinosa (2013) report.
3. Write an email, note, blog, twitter, and so on to a legislator, leader in the community, newspaper, website, social media, etc. advocating for an issue about immigrant children. What did you learn from the experience? What connections can you make with the content discussed in this course? How can this experience help you in your work with DLLs? Submit a copy of your advocacy effort and write a short reflection on the experience.

Chapter 2

Preparing Generalist Early Childhood Teachers to Work with Culturally and Linguistically Diverse Children Who Have Special Needs

Allegra Montemayor and Karen Walker

Institutions of Higher Education (IHE) have the responsibility to prepare teachers to work with exceptional children. The number of students with exceptionalities that are serviced in inclusive classrooms is increasing and preservice teachers will be responsible for their social, behavioral, and academic performance (National Center for Educational Statistics [NCES], 2017). Exceptional children may have learning and/or behavior challenges, cognitive or physical disability, or sensory impairment and could be intellectually gifted or have a special talent. Children who are culturally and linguistically diverse (CLD) can also be exceptional learners. Often teachers may not fully understand their families' values, beliefs, and traditions and/or may not be able to communicate in their primary language.

General teacher preparation programs in the United States vary in the requirements regarding skills and knowledge of exceptional children. For example, most teacher preparation programs in the State of Texas require one course with the objectives of demonstrating the following:

- Knowledge of the definition of an exceptional child,
- State and federal regulations and laws governing the exceptional child,
- Best practices in providing appropriate accommodations and instructional adaptations for children with exceptionalities in a general education classroom,
- Collaboration and consultation with multidisciplinary teams, and
- The use of technology as it relates to the instruction of students with exceptionalities.

Some of these courses embed field experiences which allow preservice teachers an opportunity to interact with exceptional children, and others do not require time spent in inclusive classrooms. In some cases, an introduction to exceptionalities course may offer experience in the field but are restricted to self-contained or separate classrooms.

As in most professions, the field of special education is full of esoteric vernacular, as demonstrated in this brief introduction. While certainly children who are CLD can be gifted or talented, our chapter is specifically devoted to understanding how generalist teachers are prepared to teach CLD children who have special needs that require educational intervention to support academic success. Students with learning and/or behavior problems, cognitive or physical disabilities, or sensory impairments require modifications to the regular curriculum or accommodations to instructional delivery methods.

Accommodations are varied but may include seating a student near the teacher and away from classroom distractions or listening to a recording instead of reading text. Or, they can be more complicated such as developing a cueing system to give a student additional processing time an opportunity to participate in class discussions or being knowledgeable of Crisis Prevention Intervention (CPI) strategies to proactively de-escalate challenging behavior. Regardless, this specific skill set is not taught to generalists preparing to teach young children and certainly not fully understood for serving students who are also CLD.

At the national level, 61% of students with disabilities are instructed in general education classrooms 80% or more of the time (USDOE, 2015). In addition, U.S. Department of Education reported that 81% of individuals ages 6–21 years that receive special education services under the Individuals with Disabilities Education Act (IDEA) spend 40% or more of their time in the general education classroom. According to *The Condition of Education 2019*, in school year 2017–18, the percentage (out of total public school enrollment) of students ages 3–21 years who received special education services under IDEA categorized by race/ethnicity were as follows:

- American Indian/Alaska Native students: 18%
- Black students: 16%
- White students and students of two or more races: 14% each
- Hispanic students: 13%
- Pacific Islander students: 11%
- Asian students: 7%

Half of these students receive services for specific learning disabilities or speech or language impairments, not necessarily disabilities requiring services delivered in a resource classroom or special school. Therefore, preservice teachers will be responsible for the education of CLD students with disabilities in their regular education classrooms.

For example, a student diagnosed with attention deficit hyperactivity disorder (ADHD) and no other disabling condition would not need to be pulled from the regular classroom, and generally should not need modifications to the curriculum. They will though require accommodations to help them be successful. To help them with organization, they may need a written schedule for daily routines or a list of goals to accomplish during the class period. If the student needs to move to improve focus, provide resistance bands on chair legs, or allow them to stand in the back of the classroom where movement would not distract other students. These accommodations do not lower academic expectations but remove barriers to learning.

Federal legislation that aligned IDEA (2004) and No Child Left Behind (2004) resulted in both student accountability and an increased attention to students with disabilities to be fully included in the general education setting. For many of those students it is the responsibility of the general education teacher to be held accountable for his/her students' academic achievement. General education teachers must have the skill set and knowledgebase to effectively educate students of special populations including CLD learners and with disabilities. The purpose of this chapter is to share how teacher preparation programs train preservice teachers to work with CLD who have special needs.

REVIEW OF EXISTING LITERATURE

Teacher preparation programs must adequately prepare general education teachers for the workforce to educate students with disabilities and that come from CLD backgrounds. There is a significant need to increase the quality of teacher preparation programs so that teachers feel like they are being effective to provide services appropriate for students from special populations.

IHE have the responsibility to be diligent in preparing teacher candidates therefore examining the preparedness for preservice teachers is crucially important especially in light of No Child Left Behind (NCLB) of 2001 and the IDEA of 2004. Federal mandates in both IDEA and NCLB state that the inclusion of students with disabilities in the general education setting and student accountability including CLD learners are becoming a general education teachers' responsibility (Mitchell & Hedge, 2007).

This section of existing literature will provide relevant literature that is twofold. First, we will explore the impact of special education laws that govern and protect students with disabilities and CLD learners. Secondly, we will explore the information that has been concluded on teacher certification program focusing on general teacher preparation programs and preparation programs specific to special populations including children who have disabilities and who are CLD.

Individuals with Disabilities Education Act

The education of students with disabilities began from a historical case involving Brown vs. Board of Education of 1954 that resulted in the Supreme Court in support for equal access and educational opportunities for all children regardless of their disability or color (Obiakor & Utley, 2004). Students with disabilities were granted with a free appropriate public education in the least restrictive environment (LRE) mandated from the original Education for All Handicapped Children Act (EAHCA) of 1975.

Prior to the EAHCA, the education of students with disabilities was the responsibility of special education teachers but today it is the responsibility of both special education and general education teachers. Students with disabilities are also to be included with their nondisabled peers to the maximum extent possible (Idol, 2006; Turnbull et al., 2009; Wright, 1999). Part of the mandate from IDEA 2004 challenges general education teachers to modify the curriculum to meet all student's needs. Therefore, the roles and responsibilities for new teachers and their role in supporting students with disabilities in the LRE must be emphasized (Van Laarhoven et al., 2007).

Teacher Education Programs

Many studies have been performed to provide evidence on the effectiveness of teacher preparation programs specific to those that plan on service students with disabilities. For example, a qualitative, correlational study investigated the relationship between preservice teacher candidates' knowledge levels and attitudes they had toward students with disabilities (Nutter, 2011). The author included eighty-eight general education preservice teacher candidates that completed their student teaching semester in Oklahoma. The participants were tasked to complete an online survey that consisted of demographic questions and the Regular Education Teacher Perceptions Survey.

This study was an investigation of the perception of preservice general education teachers regarding preparedness to teach students with special needs in the general education setting. The author explored knowledge base, skill level, and attitudes for the instruction of students with disabilities. A five-point Likert-type survey questionnaire was provided to preservice general education teacher candidates from three universities in the state of Oklahoma.

The results from this study indicated that preservice teachers have knowledge of special education laws but are not confident implementing the principles in practice. More specifically, the responses specified that preservice teachers perceive themselves to have knowledge about special education policy versus eligibility and placement procedures for students with disabilities. In addition, the findings also demonstrated that while preservice teachers perceived to be knowledgeable about an array of instructional strategies, they did not perceive themselves as knowledgeable in instructional practices as it relates to the curriculum.

Lastly, with regards to teacher skill level and policies and procedures in special education law, preservice teachers indicated that they were unable to fulfill their role as a general education teacher in the Individual Education Plan or Individualized Education Program (IEP) process. Nevertheless, they did perceive themselves as having a positive attitude toward students with disabilities, having the ability to construct measurable goals, and have the ability to monitor student progress as it related to the IEP.

Brownell et al. (2005) presented a framework to assist in analyzing teacher education programs and then used that framework to analyze practice in special education teacher preparation. The authors then used that framework that analyzed special education program descriptions and assessments in teacher education programs. The authors identified seven common features of effective teacher education program. The features included:

(a) Provide faculty with common language across all coursework and field experiences;
(b) Facilitate connections to help students link knowledge they acquire in their courses to their field experience;
(c) Carefully plan field experiences to select skilled cooperating teachers that will collaborate with faculty to streamline the support;
(d) Monitor and support preservice teacher performance;
(e) Employ active pedagogical practices to support students through modes of reflection of teaching and learning;
(f) Emphasize on students from diverse cultures and students with disabilities in placements of field experiences; and
(g) Build community across other disciplines (Brownell et al., 2005, pp. 243–244).

The methods included a review of special education teacher preparation programs in comparison to general education teacher preparation programs. Findings showed that 84% of the "programs" faculty described skillfully constructed and supervised field experiences that were tied to coursework. Next, all the program descriptions highlighted the concept of collaboration. More specifically, collaboration with the faculty was an element of 70% of the program descriptions but the nature of collaboration was not defined.

Collaboration with schools was revealed in 73% of the program descriptions and in some cases (52%), teacher educator programs indicated they used cohorts to promote collaboration.

Brownell et al. (2005) study focused on preservice teacher preparation as it relates to collaboration across field experiences. The study concluded that there needs to be a focus on skillfully constructed field experiences. The findings revealed that providing collaborative opportunities during preservice teachers' coursework between school personnel, faculty members, and other preservice teachers resulted in graduates that were more suitably prepared to teach than those that have to teach reading. Programs that support a high degree of student and faculty collaboration placing a heavy emphasis on instructional strategies and awareness for addressing diverse students can result in successful outcomes for beginning teachers.

Collaboration between general education and special education teachers is a vital skill to increase student engagement and success in the classroom. Hamilton-Jones and Vail (2014) explored undergraduate students while completing their coursework in the special education teacher program and their perceptions about collaboration between special education and general education teachers. The preservice teachers confirmed that increased student success and individualized instruction was a result of collaboration between teachers.

On the other hand, "challenges in collaboration" was a common theme among the participants including demonstrating reluctance to share instructional responsibilities within the co-teaching model. Instead, the Hamilton-Jones and Vail (2014) suggested focusing on models like parallel teaching, for example, result in a balanced power dynamic where each teacher is responsible for teaching the same content to two different heterogeneous groups of students. Nevertheless, this study proved that teacher preparation programs should provide training in the knowledge and skills necessary for collaboration.

Another facet of collaboration was discussed by Flanigan (2007) where the faculty proposed supporting preservice teachers to work and collaborate with other disciplines including majors in curriculum and instruction, elementary, and secondary education. Participants added that preservice teachers require more exposure so they can be more effective when working with students from special populations. Other levels of collaboration noted also included providing preservice teachers with parent and community partnership opportunities. It is essential to support preservice teachers to understand the impact of creating a networking system in and outside of the school with an emphasis on the parents and community (Flanigan, 2007).

Moreover, the focus on inclusion and cultural diversity was an important feature for 84% of the program descriptions (Brownell et al., 2005). The authors stated that while cultural diversity or inclusion were program topics, pedagogical practices used to help preservice teachers learn these skills were not always discussed. Twenty-eight percent contained descriptions of the methods used to help preservice teachers address the needs of CLD students with special needs and 27% discussed how faculty members supported students on topics of inclusion.

Issues regarding culture and diversity were also discussed through the findings by Flanigan (2007). Flanigan investigated 33 faculty members' experiences, attitudes, and opinions regarding preservice preparation programs through focus groups from a College of Education (COE). The faculty taught courses in curriculum and instruction, special education, and early childhood, among other disciplines. They were tasked to provide a response if teacher education programs were adequately preparing preservice teachers.

One of the key themes that emerged regarding culture is when faculty indicated that they faced challenges in expanding cultural diversity of preservice teachers who had not been exposed to cultures other than their own. This challenge was evident when preservice teachers did not understand how to interact with parents who did not speak English. This became a combination of culture and communication.

In addition, several participants felt that preservice teachers have difficulty seeing situations from the perspective of parents because they may have not had the experience of parenting. The implications from this finding require faculty members to encourage preservice teachers to view parents as vital members of a collaborative team. One of the ways to encourage collaboration, including with parents and teachers, is to teach preservice teachers to develop strong communication skills.

In Reese et al. (2018), the researchers found that many universities separate the programs of special education and general education preservice teachers. The authors explored the creation of an Urban Dual Credential Program (UDCP) in California that was meant to prepare teachers in general education and special education to work and meet the needs of CLD students and with special needs in urban school settings. This case study employed the multi-tiered systems of support (MTSS) framework that is typically used to meet the needs of students serviced in inclusion classrooms.

MTSS is based on a tiered system that identifies students who are struggling early and provides research-based interventions and data-based decisions regarding student progress. It is helpful because it encompasses both Positive Behavior Intervention and Supports (PBIS) and Response to Intervention (RtI) within a system that supports behavior and academics, respectively. In this study, MTSS was employed as the authors guiding framework for preservice teacher experiences and course development. The authors also reviewed the extent that school, district, and communities have been part of the decision-making and planning process for designing teacher preparation programs for both general education and special education preservice teachers.

The UDCP is a program that can be taken in the final two years for undergraduates seeking teacher certification in Liberal Studies or as a postbaccalaureate program that leads to dual credentials. As a result, students are required to take half of the coursework from existing programs and the other half restructured for UDCP. For example, for a student going into mathematics, Tier 1 instruction included a math methods course and added a course on intensive and targeted math interventions for Tiers 2 and 3. MTSS framework employed those same principles to guide the curriculum specific for general education and special education preservice teachers.

This framework was aligned to restructure the curriculum for UDCP in which preservice teachers completed Tiers 1, 2, and 3 courses. Tier 1 included a literacy course in their first semester where it focused on integrating oral language, writing and reading skills. Tiers 2 and 3 literacy courses that focused on reading foundations strategies during their second semester. These courses focused on the writing and reading processes and were unique to students with disabilities and for English language learners. These two courses also offered field experience.

One of the major components to UDCP experience for preservice teachers was that the courses took place in elementary school sites. During their field experiences, preservice teachers were able to work directly with students in different instructional arrangements while practicing instructional strategies. Following the fieldwork, preservice teachers were able to share their reflections and experiences with their peers and instructors once a week.

In addition, the Tiers 1, 2, and 3 courses were team taught by two general education faculty members and two special education faculty members. This was in an effort to utilize one of the service delivery models including co-teaching, which is utilized in inclusive classrooms where general education and special education teachers collaborate to support the instruction for all students. As a result, preservice teachers were able to observe the collaboration between two teachers that offered a variety of approaches and perspectives to instruction.

Another essential component to the UDCP program is that they also offered the university courses in elementary school sites where the fieldwork was completed. Preservice teachers were able to implement instructional activities to participating classroom settings while the faculty observed the implementation and allowed time for debriefing following the observations. Lastly, UDCP collaborated with the two participating school districts to provide joint professional development. This allowed for preservice teachers to participate in professional development on assistive technology, for example, held by a district-level specialist (Reese et al., 2018, p. 24).

The authors concluded that UDCP was able to transform their teacher preparation program to meet the needs of the diverse student population that includes CLD students with special needs. The ability to intertwine both theory and classroom practice within the 2-year program promoted school change and encouraged collaboration for preservice teachers. This also potentially results in retaining those quality teachers for high need school districts (Berry et al., 2008). The implementation and design of this program in collaboration with district and urban classrooms is likely to make an impact for preservice teachers and master teachers.

Successful early childhood teacher preparation programs play an integral role in preparing preservice teachers to work with young children. To illustrate, Early and Winton (2001) explored early childhood teacher preparation programs at two- and four-year IHEs. The authors noted some of the challenges that IHEs face. First, they indicated that there is a need to provide preservice teachers with field experiences of classrooms that service young children from diverse backgrounds including whom English is their second language. Secondly, the number of students with disabilities served in the inclusive and regular early childhood settings versus specialized classrooms is also a challenge that was noted.

Early and Winton (2001) concluded that a vital component to teacher preparation programs is providing proper funding and resources to improve the accessibility and quality of early childhood teacher preparation programs. As the program builds capacity other key areas include infant/toddler and content around diversity and disability is important. In addition, offer preservice teachers should have opportunities to work directly with early childhood children that come from diverse family backgrounds, cultures, and communities.

For example, offering additional experiences that require more than just completing observations but field experience or student teaching options where they work directly with the children. The authors also noted to increase the number of full-time faculty members versus part time faculty where they have more time to provide on-site mentoring to the preservice students while on the field. Lastly, in addition to recommending infrastructure updates to the faculty, the authors also concluded that there is a need for diversity both racial and cultural within the faculty that educates students in hopes that it will motivate them to pursue advanced degrees.

Teacher preparation programs have an obligation to better prepare general education teachers for students with disabilities in their classrooms. To support this claim, Lombardi and Hunka (2001) reviewed the West Virginia University's 5-year preservice teacher education program and provided evidence from national and state data regarding identification and placement of students with disabilities in the United States.

These findings support the need for general education teachers to have the skills to provide modifications and accommodations to meet the individualized needs of their students. Indeed, it is necessary to better prepare general education teachers for students with disabilities in their classrooms. A survey questionnaire of open and closed-ended questions was completed by seventy-two West Virginia University preservice teachers majoring in elementary or secondary education. Other participants included eleven faculty members that were responsible for teaching core courses in the program specific to general education.

The purpose of Lombardi and Hunka (2001) study was to obtain information regarding the level of confidence and competence the participants felt about the strand approach. The strand approach was developed by the university which included ten outcomes and 28 competencies for areas including special education, technology, and multiculturalism included into all core courses required in the teacher preparation program. More specifically, this included students majoring in elementary or secondary teacher education.

These outcomes and competencies developed for the area of special education were recommendations from existing literature and by the Council of Exceptional Children (1995). The outcomes specific to children with special needs included different areas of expertise and knowledge including expertise and knowledge of children, learning, assessment, supportive and safe learning environments, instructional effectiveness, collaborative relationships, working with paraprofessionals, planning and implementation of individualized education plan, transition plan, and school's strategic plan as it relates to exceptional children (Lombardi & Hunka, 2001, pp. 194–195).

As the preservice teachers advanced through the program, Lombardi and Hunka (2001) hypothesized that they would gradually learn all learning outcomes and competencies and increase their confidence levels for teaching in inclusive classrooms. The authors assessed the confidence and competence levels of both students and faculty before the fifth year of the program. Results showed that as preservice students advanced into the later years of the West Virginia University's teacher education program that their learning of special education outcomes and competencies did strengthen. It also demonstrated that adding a special education strand to the program that provided some degree of effectiveness to preservice teachers with information suitable to working with students with disabilities.

Despite this important finding it is important to note that 25% of the students that completed their fourth year reported neither competent nor confident to teach students with special needs in inclusive classrooms. On the other hand, 48% of second year students reported feeling both a lack of confidence and competence. These findings show that the focus of preservice programs should be on not only acquiring knowledge but also using the knowledge in practical ways closest to the fifth and final year of the program. This includes the internship which should be heavily emphasized for working with students with special needs.

As a result, Lombardi and Hunka (2001) noted that since the preservice students indicated they desired for additional hands-on experiences with students with disabilities, the authors recommended that their clinical teaching experiences continue to emphasize the special education outcomes and competencies. Additionally, the authors recommended that preservice teachers are offered opportunities to not just observe but to engage with students with disabilities during their clinical teaching experiences. Lastly, the authors offered a strong recommendation to design an additional special education course specific to just general education preservice teachers rather than using a course specially designed for special education majors or minors (Lombardi & Hunka, 2001).

Summary

Federal special education law requires that all students, including those with disabilities receive a free and appropriate education in the LRE. It also requires that students with disabilities and who are CLD are making adequate progress in their academic achievement. Existing literature supports the need for quality teacher preparation programs. More specifically, the importance of designing a successful program that offers coursework specific to the areas of instructional strategies including co-teach models, collaboration with instructional staff (i.e. paraprofessionals), parental involvement, and on-site mentoring and coaching from university faculty during clinical teaching and student teaching.

DISCUSSION

Based on personal education and experiences in special education classrooms, conversations with colleagues in the field, and a review of published research, most preservice generalists do not feel that they were adequately prepared to work with CLD students who have special needs. In fact, some have stated the wish of having more time to take additional courses in exceptionalities. Several points of interest were mentioned:

Teaching in Silos

At most IHE in the State of Texas, one course covering vast and varied objectives is required. Some require none, and offer courses focused on exceptional children as electives. In our experience, one colleague mentioned that the concept of teaching exceptional children should not be taught as a stand-alone course but should be embedded in all teacher preparation courses. The integration of inclusion and diversity as threads across all standards is a noble goal, but all IHE faculty may not have the experience and expertise to teach the skills and knowledge necessary to work with exceptional children.

It is important to encourage IHE teacher preparation programs to offer coursework where general education faculty works with special education faculty so that preservice teachers receive both levels of expertise. The idea of co-planning involving a variety of disciplines may be an undertaking at the collegial level however if the faculty can find a common ground and understanding that each share unique perspectives it can be a rich and meaningful experience for preservice teachers.

Perhaps some of the findings from the Brownell et al. (2005) study could be utilized to break the silos. Provide faculty with common language across all coursework and place emphasis on students from diverse cultures and students with disabilities in placements of field experiences. Follow inclusion model from public schools—partner faculty with knowledge of special education with methods faculty.

As in Reese et al. (2018), many teacher preparation programs separate general education and special education, further creating silos and isolation. Many of the strategies utilized to create modifications and accommodations can be useful with general education students who may be struggling with content or instruction delivery falling in RtI Tier 1 or Tier 2.

Classroom Management versus Individual Student Management

CLD students with special needs children do not always respond to the classroom management strategies utilized in general education classrooms, those processes that help ensure that schedules, routines, and lessons run smoothly. IHE should also prepare teachers in managing individual student behavior, those students who come to class feeling not understood, having a special need, or having faced an adverse childhood experience. For these children, we should not ask, "What is wrong with this child?" but should ask, "What has happened to this child?"

Collaboration and Consultation

General education and special education teachers have the shared responsibility to communicate and collaborate with each other as a multidisciplinary team. It is for the development and effective use of research-based strategies for students with special needs. Preservice teachers may not understand that it will be their responsibility to address the individualized needs of their students in an inclusive setting.

Some teachers have reported that they have felt ill-prepared when working with special education teachers which are barriers that prevent collaboration. In addition, preservice teachers may not have had the opportunity to observe collaborative efforts with respect to IEP meetings due to lack of opportunity for this field experience. Preservice teachers need to learn that the education of all children is a collaborative effort.

Nutter (2011) found that teachers had knowledge of special education laws but were not confident implementing the principles in practice. Teachers felt they were able to develop measurable goals and monitor student progress as it relates to the IEP. Methods for Brownell et al. (2005) revealed that providing collaborative opportunities across field experiences that emphasize instructional strategies and awareness for addressing diverse students can result in successful outcomes for beginning educators.

Paraprofessionals

Paraprofessionals that provide direct support to students with special needs work under the supervision of a teacher. Ultimately, it is the responsibility of the general education teacher to meet with the special education teacher on a regular basis to provide information on accommodations and adaptations and how the paraprofessional can support the designated tasks in the inclusive classroom. Preservice teachers may not have had the opportunity to learn about how to consult and collaborate with special education support staff including paraprofessionals and how these roles are defined.

The lack of opportunity to observe these roles can affect preservice teacher attitudes about working with special education staff. IHE faculty can assist in facilitating the collaboration with the schools that host preservice teachers and discuss ways that the mentor teachers can include preservice teachers in the collaboration that occurs among special education staff.

Parents and Families

The recognition of including parents and families in the education of children who are linguistically and culturally diverse and have special needs is of critical importance. IHE should strongly consider adding a required course on how to work with families and viewing families as partners in the areas of communication, development of individualized education plans, and partners for successful student outcomes. Some preservice teachers may feel that it is difficult to understand the perspectives of parents of children who have special needs that would have been afforded to them if they had field experience hours.

Flanigan (2007) supports this evidence by indicating that collaboration is required to happen between teachers, parents, and other professionals involved in working with the child. To illustrate, she discussed focusing on communication with parents as part of the course work including requiring parent conferences during clinical teaching and student teaching experiences. These experiences include role playing, a discussion of seating arrangement during a conference, or offer preservice teachers to attend Parent-Teacher Association (PTA) meetings.

If preservice teachers do not have the opportunity to do field experiences in their teacher preparation program they will not have the chance to observe what a meaningful home-school partnership looks like. IHE should also consider focusing on the importance of partnerships with parents and how teachers must take the initiative to provide a warm and open atmosphere and encourage involvement (Flanigan, 2007).

Professional Development

In addition to IHE preparation for preservice teachers, there is a vast amount of existing literature that confirms the need to provide early childhood teachers with continued in-service opportunities. There is a strong connection between professional development of teachers and increased levels of student achievement, demonstrating a strong link to improving pedagogical practices (Reese et al., 2018).

For special education teachers, IHE preparation programs tend to focus on equipping special education teachers to work in specialized settings including self-contained or separate classrooms. However, today's special education teachers are expected to collaborate and consult with general education teachers to support students with diverse needs including students with diverse cultural and linguistic needs and across varied levels of support, while still providing specially designed instruction (Brownell et al., 2010).

In addition to the collaboration that occurs with general education teachers, special education teachers are expected to have knowledge of content, grade level standards, stay current in the knowledge base in special education, strategies on how to work with parents and families of their students with disabilities, and be in tune with new technology (Shepherd et al., 2016). This level of collaboration across university and school districts was evident in Reese et al. (2018) through their UDCP. This program was able to embed literacy and math courses while preservice teachers were exposed to the co-teach model.

This exposure allowed for a variety of instructional interventions and approaches. Another vital recommendation taken from the program is for

IHE to partner with school districts that host our preservice teachers so that they are involved in professional development opportunities offered to school staff.

CONCLUSION AND RECOMMENDATIONS

As more districts move to make classrooms inclusive, the need for general education teachers who have both the knowledge and ability to teach CLD who have special needs is more critical today than ever before. More studies are needed that investigate how IHE and teacher preparation programs adequately train preservice teachers to work with CLD who have special needs in order to better create programmatic change. We deem it necessary to focus on children with special needs considering the increase of students with disabilities in the general education classrooms.

Examples from Practice

In this section, we have included a few examples of assignments that could be incorporated in different courses to address the knowledge, skills, and dispositions described in this chapter.

1. Add courses that focus on inclusive pedagogy in teacher preparation programs.
2. Transform teacher preparation programs to look more like the schools in the community.
3. Collaborate with faculty within teacher preparation programs to provide professional development regarding children with exceptionalities.
4. Add required field experiences for preservice teachers in inclusive and self-contained classrooms.

Chapter 3

Preservice Teacher Confessions
"Why Should I Care about Parents?"
Tivy Nobles Whitlock

Preservice teachers often enter the profession unaware of the scope and number of mindful communication exchanges that must take place with parents in working with children. Empathic skills are part of mindful communication and may influence the ability of preservice teachers to effectively communicate with parents (Peck et al., 2015; Whitlock, 2019). The practice of empathy is critical for future teachers because it can help foster authentic conversation.

Empathy involves treating others with care, respect, and dignity, and to be mindful of our words and how we use them. Empathy can also act as a catalyst to help build a culture of community between teachers and parents (Brown et al., 2009). This is particularly important if we want to ensure that all kinds of diversity are acknowledged such as in the case of families who are CLD, those who have children with special needs, and are of different structure.

USING EMPATHY AS A STIMULUS FOR AUTHENTIC LEARNING AND TRANSFORMATION

Teaching should be responsive and help students connect to what is happening in the world around them, taking into consideration and being sensitive to influences from their home and their neighborhood. In order for a transformative learning shift to occur, preservice teachers have to be able to recognize the position of privilege they have been afforded as an educator (Apple et al., 2009). Empathy can help to create an equitable balance for this power of privilege. Educators must not have a "savior mentality" but one that respects and values others.

Empathic skills can heighten awareness for preservice teachers of the inequities that exist in delivering instruction to marginalized children of color and families in poverty. Empathy can also act as a self-regulating agent that holds preservice teachers to greater accountability (Giroux, 2004). Real learning occurs when preservice teachers are willing and open-minded to practicing empathy to become critical thinking-minded educators.

STUDYING EMPATHY AND THE PRESERVICE TEACHER

The Early Childhood Teacher Self-Reflection Model or EC-TSR (see chapter 4) was developed to mentor preservice teachers to learn to work with parents. Preservice teachers enrolled in a child development course in a Hispanic Serving Institution (HSI) were asked to participate in a family literacy program for 6 weeks. The model focused on mentoring students through reflection journals that asked specific questions about working with parents in an early literacy program provided by a local grocer (see chapter 4).

After several semesters of implementing the model in a child development course, the emerging theme of "empathy" across the preservice teachers' journal reflections was noted. As such, to better understand their notions, it was decided to incorporate intentional questions to the existing questions in the reflective journal that would help all students reflect on empathy toward families. Listening to preservice teachers is crucial in order better prepare them to work with parents. Effective listening is crucial in order to know preservice teachers' thinking.

In order to better analyze the theme of empathy, a qualitative case study was developed to investigate how empathy influences preservice teachers' beliefs about parents. One section of a child development course served as the setting for the study with 29 participants. The course was part of the teacher preparation program. Of the 29 participants, 26 (90%) were female and 3 (10%) were male and the majority of the students were of Latinx descent.

In order to increase preservice teachers' knowledge of working with families, a field experience component was added to the course syllabus. The six-week field experience component includes the family literacy program sponsored by a local grocer (see chapter 4). The focus of the program is to help to increase the literacy experiences and nutrition of underserved populations. Preservice teachers used the curriculum provided by the education department of the sponsoring business. The curriculum was developed to guide parents in the process of early literacy development and nutrition.

Since this was the first time most of the preservice teachers had ever worked with parents, it was important for them to receive information on important topics about parents and families. Each week a researcher visited the class during their scheduled class for a 30-minute lesson based on one of the six topics from the enhanced EC-TSR mentoring model (see chapter 4): *Getting Started, Communication, Cultural Awareness, Parenting Styles, Learning Styles, Family Values,* and *Final Reflections.*

The lessons were guided by the National Association for the Education of Young Children or NAEYC DAP Standards. The researcher provided guidance to the preservice teachers to increase participant knowledge and learning about families as a form of professional development. At the end of each week, the preservice teachers responded to reflection questions posted on an online platform.

The journal reflections were analyzed for empathy themes using naturalistic inquiry to yield generalizable findings that can be applied to broader contexts and nurture greater understanding of the phenomenon (Lincoln & Guba, 1985; Melrose, 2010; Stake, 1995). The objective was to listen to preservice teacher self-reflections for emphatic thinking toward families. This in turn provided information for teacher preparation programs to build empathic thinking that is needed in order to enhance communication with parents.

The guiding research question was: How does professional development with preservice teachers help strengthen empathic relationships and potentially enhance communication with parents of pre-school age children? Two major categories were used to analyze the data and each category had three-five different themes. The first category encompassed communication and it included the themes of words, nonverbal communication, and tone of voice. The second category was empathy and the themes included welcoming, vulnerability, perspective taking, and awareness of bias.

FINDINGS

The top five themes that emerged in the study to better prepare preservice teachers in building empathic communication with parents included (1) welcoming, (2) vulnerability, (3) perspective taking, (4) willingness, and (5) awareness of bias. The participant direct responses were transcribed verbatim to maintain authenticity. Each of the themes will be described below.

Welcoming

Welcoming refers to a positive demonstration of acceptance, such as establishing a safe space where parents feel like they belong and can openly engage with teachers to ensure that each child achieves academic success (Ball, 2006; Dotger, 2009; Epstein, 2011; McKenna & Millen, 2013; Nieto, 2009). Data revealed that the preservice teachers were excited about the opportunity of participating in the professional development model (EC-TSR) to acquire first-hand experience connecting with parents.

The preservice teachers not only talked about wanting to get to know the parents, but they also expressed wanting to learn how to communicate with parents and hear their viewpoints.

For example, Carlos wrote, "I am looking forward to meeting the parents and their children. I feel as if I will learn new things from them. I am also eager to create new relationships and possibly make a difference and impact the lives of these families." The overall feeling expressed from the participants seemed to be that of appreciation for being able to have an opportunity to experience talking with parents in the early stage of their career.

Similar comments from the participants were expressed in class discussions and noted this in the researcher field notes. Smiles and nods of the head were observed as the class engaged in conversation on this topic. The preservice teachers talked about wanting to get to know the parents. They expressed wanting to learn how to communicate with parents and hear their viewpoints.

Maria shared in her journal, "The thing I am most looking forward to is getting able to discuss information with parents and hear their perspectives. So often, as teachers, we're used to spreading knowledge on subjects and keeping limited conversations with other adults, but now we get to hear what parents are interested in and what their opinions are." There were many references made across the students' reflection journals that were welcoming to parents.

The preservice teachers also discussed the importance of having empathy, and respecting parents and what parents have to say. Yolanda shared, "It is important that they (parents) feel respected and comfortable enough to be themselves." Stephanie shared similar reflections in her journal, "(empathy) is important because the last thing I would want is for the parents to feel like they are not important or what they have to say is not important." It was interesting to see that while working directly with parents, the preservice teachers tried to put themselves in the shoes of the parents and connected to how they themselves would want to be treated.

By embracing and being welcoming of parents, the preservice teachers gained valuable, new insight and inspiration to build collaborations with parents. These critical connections would not be able to take place if the preservice teachers were afraid to work with parents. Bella said, "Empathy is definitely something that should take place in my future classroom. . . . It helped me see how parents aren't something to be worried about when teaching. They should be seen as our partners in giving their child the education they deserve." This shows Bella's willingness to understand the role of the parent.

The preservice teachers journaled about how professional development was needed to help them grow and understand that they share the same goal as parents. Another key finding revealed how professional development was an important factor in helping reduce fears in communicating and working with parents. These findings show that preservice teachers must be able to understand parents in order to know how to best make them feel welcome.

Vulnerability

Vulnerability is at the core of communication, and it is a bridge for authentic, meaningful connections with others (Brown, 2015; Decety & Jackson, 2004). Vulnerability is a state of being open to share about yourself and being genuinely open to experiencing feelings (Epstein, 2011). Through reflective journaling, the preservice teachers were able to open up and share feelings they were experiencing as they worked with parents. Journals became a platform for preservice teachers to show their vulnerability.

One of the major findings of the study was that the preservice teachers were afraid to initially work with the parents. Barbara was one of several participants who expressed this in her journal. She said, "My biggest fear is working with parents. I know it is something we have to do, but I am nervous." Data revealed that a major reason connected to the fear was a feeling of being judged. For example, Kaitlin said, "A fear that I do have after being told the parents will be there is parents being judgmental. I fear that the parents will not listen to me since I'm very young and I don't know what I'm talking about." The fear comes from not knowing what to expect.

Some of the preservice teachers openly discussed feeling a fear of being judged due to their age. They wanted to know what the magic answer was to getting parents to respect them. Henrietta also wrote about this in her journal expressing, "My fear is that the parents wont [sic] treat me with respect or that I come off trying to be better than them. I want to help them but don't want to do it the wrong way." The fear of being judged comes from feeling insecure about something in this case the preservice teachers' notions of respect and doing things right.

Findings revealed that several of the preservice teachers were afraid of being judged by the parents simply because they were not parents themselves or they did not have kids. For example, Dalen wrote in his journal, "I know that it is intimidating but I know that having to talk to those who have kids when I don't is going to be hard." Despite having these fears and concerns, the preservice teachers were not afraid to be vulnerable and put themselves out there or even fail.

The participants self-reported that when they were honest with the parents and openly shared their own weaknesses, it yielded positive results and helped bring them closer to the parents. In Adriana's journal she wrote, "I think being honest with them that I can't dance or I don't eat right 100% allowed them to open up and relax a little more." Being honest with themselves helped bridged being honest with the parents.

A key contributing factor is that the preservice teachers were open to being vulnerable (and allowing others to see some of their imperfections) in a safe environment. While in class discussions, as well, the preservice teachers talked about how being open to experiencing feelings helped them to develop connections with parents and see things from a different lens. Many of the participants shared they were surprised to learn that the parents gave them positive feedback and were actually supportive of them and should not be feared.

Yolanda was one of the participants who expressed this viewpoint in her journal. She wrote, "This program helped me come out of my shell a lot more and not be so nervous talking with parents. It gave me a better insight on how parents actually are and how supportive they are." When the preservice teachers allowed themselves to be vulnerable in working with parents, they discovered that they had a lot in common with the parents which created a sense of support.

Perspective Taking

Perspective taking means being able to understand multiple perspectives that are different from your own and acknowledge and appreciate differences in others (Brown, 2015; Decety & Jackson, 2004). This is not always easy to do in a new situation. For many preservice teachers it is the first time that they actually go to a different neighborhood that may be diverse economically, culturally, linguistically, and of immigrant status. Although the majority of the students are Latinx, some may not relate to the parents' experiences as they may be of different generation.

Again, for most of these preservice teachers, they had never worked with parents before. Adding to the anxiety and stress was their age. Most of the participants were between ages 20 and 25. They self-reported that they were not a parent and they did not have children. Imagine the fear on the first day of class learning you're going to be placed in an authoritative, professional capacity over parents to teach them about early literacy and nutrition. The preservice teachers felt intimidated and scared.

However, data supported that the preservice teachers were able to put themselves in the shoes of the parents and reflect on possible feelings and fears that parents might have. For example, Dalen wrote in his journal, "I also feel like the parents are equally nervous about going into something new and not knowing what to expect. I need to be sensitive to this and realize that this is new to everyone!" Karen shared similar statements writing, "I think the parents are scared to ask questions if they don't understand what we are trying to teach them." It was evident that the students began to understand the parents.

A significant finding from the study was that perspective taking allowed the preservice teachers to understand that parents do not see or hear what happens in the classroom and this may cause some parents to worry if their child does not have a caring and supportive teacher. This is a very important concept to for preservice teachers to understand as they will be working with families and need to know families' expectations and fears.

The preservice teachers like Kaitlin, seemed to validate the parents' fears. In Kaitlin's journal she wrote,

> I think fears some parents may have are us future teachers encouraging and believing in their child. . . . Parents want their child to be supported and encouraged in order to achieve and I feel that parents fear they child(s) [sic] aren't receiving that kind of support system from educator. . . . As educators it is important for us to know that we don't all share the same perceptions as each others [sic]. Its [sic] important to let children know that it is okay to different from others, that is what makes each of us unique.

Kaitlin showed her understanding of the importance of seeing differences in each other.

Many of the preservice teachers were able to consider and validate that parents may have perspectives different from their own. Some of the participants were also able to self-reflect on factors that might hinder their communication efforts with parents. For example, Carlos wrote,

> not all parents can become involved in their children's education because of the language barrier. It's crucial to find a way to communicate effectively with parents, especially in a language they understand. . . . With knowing my own learning style, I need to remind myself that everyone learns differently and some parents may not have the same perspective as I do.

Although Carlos acknowledged how language barriers can deter parent involvement, he firmly stated the importance of communicating with parents in their language thus providing an asset-based perception of the parents' cultural heritage.

Findings from the study showed that empathy acted as a catalyst and created a pathway for the preservice teachers to approach this assignment not with the intention to lecture parents, but to collaborate and talk with parents. Isabella is one of the participants who shared this viewpoint. She said, "I know sometimes that teachers can jump to conclusions and think parents [sic]. And their perception may or may not be correct. Before a teacher jumps to conclusions it is important to talk to the parent." This statement is crucial particularly when working with diverse parents.

The ability to acknowledge that there are multiple perceptions within a diverse group of parents fostered a greater awareness of multiple realities and multiple truths (Baum, 2005; Stake, 1995). The preservice teachers not only were able to construct meaning through these social interactions, but some also transcended from old, harmful perspectives and behaviors perhaps even from racist views.

Willingness

Willingness is much more than a state of being ready (Brown, 2015). The power of willingness propels intrinsic self-motivation that causes one to act. In this study, the preservice teachers journaled and talked about their willingness to act after receiving information from professional development. Some of the participants expressed feeling surprised to learn something that they may have considered to be a small act actually made a big difference in communicating with parents.

Many of the participants also felt that prior to the professional development, they didn't pay attention or they were not aware of how their words and behaviors affected conversations. Patricia explained,

> With my own parents, there have been times when I say something while making a certain face or making a hand gesture in response to what my parents have told me and I've gotten in trouble all for something I didn't even say out loud. . . . I know how important non-verbal communication is and the effects it has on the conversation your [sic] having.

This perception shows how professional development can deter harmful behaviors towards parents.

The preservice teachers were presented with an opportunity to practice willingness to think and act differently in their communication with parents. It is important to note how the preservice teachers reflected based on their own experience. The outcome of these teachable moments was visible immediately. Interestingly, some of the preservice teachers indicated that the parents could tell if they were being sincere or not in their conversations.

Being aware of what others are thinking and feeling is a good indication that the preservice teachers cared about learning from the parents. Gabriela, for example, said, "One experience I had with the parents from this project so far was that when I was asking them questions to get them involved, some of them were not as enthused to give a response, and I think it was because they could tell I was just trying to get my information out." A major contributing factor in how a communication message is received is associated with whether or not the other party views it as being genuine. It was important that the preservice teacher recognized this because it will help her improve her communication with parents.

This study showed that being willing to engage in new ways of communication, reduced stress and helped the preservice teachers enjoy teaching the parenting sessions. Stephanie was one of the participants who shared this viewpoint. In her journal, she wrote, "I learned that the more comfortable you are with yourself the more comfortable you will be with the parents and most importantly with the students." This is another example of the importance that preservice teachers felt about been honest and transparent.

When the preservice teachers felt comfortable, they were better able to make parents make stronger connections and understanding of the text. For example, Adriana shared in her journal, "I quickly learned that focusing on things, places, foods or basically anything that they are familiar with will get them talking and make them more comfortable . . . and allow them to open up; creating that bond." Similarly, Mia wrote, "I learned from the parents about what is important in their lives and it gave me framework to create and suggest activities they could be doing at home. For some of the families, making dinner together was important. This was a great time to tell stories as well as bring in other subjects."

The preservice teachers were able to recognize and appreciate that parents bring a lot of knowledge and have had a lot of valuable experiences. The participants talked about the importance of not just giving parents information, but letting parents talk and piggy back off each other (Donohue, 2017; Epstein, 2011). As a result, the preservice teachers learned that as the parents became more engaged, they wanted to know more. Being willing to engage in mutual, two-way communication, helped the preservice teachers create a safe, welcoming space for parents that promoted successful dialogue.

Awareness of Bias

The final emergent theme identified from the study was an awareness of bias. Preservice teachers have to be aware of what they think (Brown, 2015). If a teacher says or does something that may be perceived as offensive or prejudiced on the basis of race, color, religion, sex, age, national origin, veteran status, sexual orientation, gender identity, disability, or any other basis of discrimination prohibited by law, he or she first has to be aware of it. No change can occur or the individual cannot do anything about it unless he or she is aware of the bias.

For example, let's take a closer look at one of the preservice teacher journals. John is a 27-year old male who chose not to disclose his race. However, he did self-disclose that he speaks English-only and he comes from a family where both parents had some college. In one of John's early journal entries, he wrote,

> Culture is the worst way of looking at things. Yes, everyone is different but I do not think that culture needs to be a concern when teaching different children. Every child will be taught in the same specific manner with no favoritism. The families at my location are people. They eat, sleep, and breathe like everyone else. I would say the only thing that might be of concern is language and different speakers. Since we are in a dual-language society, it is difficult to understand many children when they do not speak your predominant language.

This finding was consistent with the literature. Deficit thinking may cause some teachers to falsely believe they know what is best for parents and think that it is their job to undo what has been done in the home (Solorzano et al., 2000). It is not always easy to accept the practices of other families as valid and important, especially when these practices may be different from your own or those practiced by you. This type of bias will also lead to conflict with parents (Ball, 2006).

As John continued to participate in the professional development model, he often talked about how he learned a great deal about parents whose backgrounds were much different from his own. By directly working parents, it gave him a chance to see that he shared some things in common with the parents. Although none of the other preservice teachers (or the researcher) shared John's belief that a student's culture is not important, John's honest reflections were very important in the findings of this study.

For example, John wrote in his journal, "It is quite upsetting to see so few nuclear families now, due to whatever kinds of situations occurred." This data provides valuable insight as to the range of influences that prevent teachers from working with parents and more research can be done in this area. It also reinforces the need for effective parent engagement strategies because the families that will require the most support from teachers are those that are marginalized (Donohue, 2017). If there is any disconnect with minority or low socioeconomic families, it can foster a negative belief that culture, class, or even linguistic history are connected to intellectual capacity (Ball, 2006). In this case, the disconnect was with being biased against families of different structures.

Once preservice teachers become aware of their biases, they are now responsible to act and make decisions in the best interest of the student. John acknowledged that he was aware of his biases. However, being responsible for our decisions and our actions is a choice. If teachers fail to accept this responsibility, it will hinder parent engagement. Interestingly, John never communicated that his perception changed but at least this course made him aware of his own biases. The hope is that other courses and professional development throughout the program can indeed help him change such deficit perceptions.

Empathic communication skills are an invaluable asset needed to better prepare preservice teachers to engage with parents that identify with cultural backgrounds different than their own (Dotger, 2009). Empathy-focused professional development can lessen the creation of an "us versus them" mentality and promote a welcoming, safe, and equitable environment where teachers mutually collaborate with parents to ensure where every child succeeds (Nieto, 2009; McKenna & Millen, 2013; Whitlock, 2019).

CONCLUSION AND RECOMMENDATIONS

Empathy plays a significant role in one's ability to nurture authentic conversations. It is a required skill for teachers because they are responsible for the care and well-being of young children; but, also because it's significant element that can increase trust and respect, and communicate value to parents. When parents are actively engaged in their child's school, it supports the work of teachers. Parents are the child's first teacher and they are vital in the growth and development of young children (Epstein, 2011; Garrett, 2009).

Teachers must learn how to work with diverse parents that look and talk very different than they do. Effective teacher communication skills are more critical than ever (Ball, 2006; Dotger, 2009). Everyone has a story. Our lived experiences and knowledge represent multiple truths and multiple realities that should be appreciated rather than feared.

Professional development is a valuable tool that can help preservice teachers enhance their funds of knowledge on engaging families (Moll et al., 1992). It also provides a multitude of opportunities for teachers to continually enhance and update critical core competencies like empathy in order to effectively communicate with parents (Hansen-Thomas et al., 2016). One major advantage of professional development is that it can create a non-threatening space where preservice teachers can practice newly learned skills working side-by-side with parents; most importantly, before they formally enter the classroom. Strong parent-teacher relationships increase student success (Epstein & Sanders, 2006).

Teacher preparation programs are an ideal outlet to incorporate empathy-focused, specialized professional development to prepare teacher candidates to work with parents. This transformative approach challenges higher level thinking as a guide for conversations and informed decisions. Empathic communication skills foster authentic conversation and a pathway to new ideas that can assist preservice teachers who might be working with parents for the first time. Positive learning environments can promote collaboration between teachers and parents and build a culture of support (Brown et al., 2009).

Teachers play a lead role in strengthening conversations with parents and growing parent engagement. This fosters an environment where everyone socially interacts and learns from one another. Teachers learn from students and parents, just as students and parents learn from teachers. Critical empathic communication skills take time to develop. Professional development on this subject can help teachers continually enhance and update their skills. Early childhood educators have the power to disrupt outdated discourse by creating an environment where empathy is the norm.

Suggestions for Practice

In this section, we have included a few examples of assignments that could be incorporated in different courses to address the knowledge, skills, and dispositions described in this chapter.

1. Examine the teacher preparation program to determine if socio-emotional issues such as empathy are present.
2. Develop a preservice teacher needs assessment survey to determine what the students feel they need regarding the issue of empathy.
3. Provide professional development for faculty regarding issues of race in order to determine their empathy stance toward children and families of color and those with disabilities or exceptionalities.
4. Create focus groups among the faculty in the teacher preparation program to listen to each other discuss the meaning of empathy and their feelings about empathy toward preservice teachers.
5. Watch the following TED Talk video https://www.youtube.com/watch?v=u5GCetbP7Fg. Reflect on how the video relates to the situation in teacher preparation programs. How are issues of race related to empathy?

Chapter 4

The Early Childhood Teacher Self-Reflection Model*

Mari Riojas-Cortez and Tivy Nobles Whitlock

In order to create a strong community of learners, teachers must know the families they serve. The NAEYC has recently revised its Professional Preparation Standards and Competencies including Standard 2 that focuses on working with families. Learning to work with families is not as easy as it sounds. Early childhood teachers in training or preservice teachers need models to help them lay the foundation for future development of healthy, productive, collaborative partnerships with the most important people in children's lives: their family.

The Early Childhood Teacher Self-Reflection Model was developed for preservice early childhood teachers enrolled in a teacher preparation program at a HSI in South Central Texas. The process for developing this model provides faculty in teacher preparation programs a template that can be adjusted depending on the context. Furthermore, the model can be used not only with preservice teachers but also with new childcare teachers and other early childhood professionals. By developing a model, we target the urgent need for preservice teachers (and others) to take action and be ready to develop partnerships with families.

BACKGROUND

We are a HSI in South Central Texas in a city of about 1.5 million people. The U.S. Census American Community Survey (2016) estimates that 63.6% of our population is Latino or Hispanic with the majority being of Mexican descent. Families comprise about 48.3% of the city's population. About 44%

---

* With appreciation to Dr. Raquel Cataldo for her contribution to the model.

of families speak Spanish in the home this is not surprising due to the historical background of the city and its proximity with Mexico.

Although our city attracts many families, the literacy and education rates remain low. Families are usually employed in minimum-wage jobs such as in restaurants and hotels. The median household income is about $46,744 and 29% of children under the age of 18 live under the poverty line. All of these statistics are important to note as the majority of our university students come from our communities and the rest also come from similar communities outside of the city.

OUR STUDENTS

Our university students mirror our local community. Fifty-three percent are Latino, 24% are White, 9% Black, and the rest comprise additional ethnicities. The majority of our students are first generation and are on financial aid. Our students are very admirable, as they have to manage many life experiences while trying to finish their undergraduate degree. The majority of our students work outside the university setting with many working over 30 hours a week.

In addition, many of our students have children and other family obligations such as taking care of ailing parents and other issues affecting family members. Nevertheless, they show their commitment to their education by participating in required field experiences, as they want to learn more about children and their families (although they usually do not think about working with parents when they begin their teacher preparation program).

COMMUNITY STAKEHOLDERS INTEREST IN LITERACY

In 2011, one of our local grocers initiated a family literacy program to encourage families to read with their young children while also learning about proper nutrition. The program is based on the belief that when families read to children, they help them develop the necessary skills to be successful in school. The lessons focus on early literacy and nutrition. The family literacy program created a 12-week[1] lesson plan to incorporate the everyday chores into learning experiences. This resembles previous research regarding the connection between learning and home experiences (i.e. Riojas-Cortez et al., 2001).

The children that attend the family literacy program are usually not enrolled in school and are about 3-years-old but many families bring their other younger children as they are welcome to do so, although there are some locations where the children enrolled in school participate in the program. The idea is to reach out to families and increase the literacy experiences in the home by attending workshops but also by having the opportunity increase the number of books available in children's homes, something of great importance due to the low literacy rates of the city.

In addition, there is a significant need to combat the high rate of childhood obesity in our city as such this program also focuses culturally relevant nutritious meals. Employees from the local grocery store volunteer to attend the workshop and share with parents the part of the lesson that focuses on nutrition. Of great importance is that the curriculum is also offered in Spanish and the lessons reflect the culture of the local families.

COMMUNITY PARTNERSHIPS

An important aspect of this family literacy program is the partnerships across the community. In our case, the local grocery store contacted our institution of higher education to see if we could find student volunteers to work with the parents and the children. Since we shared similar goals regarding literacy and working with parents we were happy to do more than just volunteer work but create a partnership. Faculty who were teaching a child development course in our teacher preparation program wanted the experience to be more than volunteer work and it was incorporated as service learning volunteer work.

The organization of the model is as follows. The preservice teachers attend the family literacy program once a week for six weeks and are provided the curriculum developed by the educational coordinator from the local grocery store. Each session is divided into two hours and includes literacy and nutrition lessons. The preservice teachers review the lessons to share with the parents. The grocery store provides the curriculum, materials, books, food, and at the end of the workshop a $25 gift card valid at the grocery store.

A coordinator and lead teacher is provided by the setting to help the preservice teachers with logistics. The grocery store provides "partners" that are responsible for teaching the nutrition lessons which include easy-to-follow cooking ideas that are culturally relevant. The partners work together with the preservice teachers to ensure that the lessons are organized and follow a logical flow.

As we began our partnership, however, we quickly realized that we needed to be more intentional with our preservice teachers regarding working with parents. The intentionality would lead the second author (and another former doctoral student) to develop the Early Childhood Teacher Self-Reflection Model or EC-TSR under the guidance of the first author.

50   Mari Riojas-Cortez and Tivy Nobles Whitlock

LEARNING ABOUT FAMILIES

The professional preparation standards of the NAEYC (2018) indicate that "candidates prepared in early childhood degree programs understand that successful early childhood education depends upon partnerships with children's families and communities." However, in order for preservice teachers to develop this understanding, they must reflect on their *perceptions* of parents before they can discover how they feel about *working* with parents. This is also true for new childcare educators.

Working with parents is an abstract concept for the majority of the preservice teachers and as such they must experience it in order to understand it. Since we wanted our students to have a positive experience, we decided to take a step back and create a systematic way of guiding students to gain a positive understanding of the meaning of working with families particularly because the majority of the families involved in the literacy program are of color and of low-income background.

The process is important because it shows the need to provide students with professional development in order to succeed particularly when working with parents. It also provides a template for other programs to develop a program that would best fit their needs. Figure 4.1 shows the process that occurred before the creation of the model. Noteworthy is, that it is not sufficient to base field experiences on standards, it is important to review the standards and examine students' understanding in order to have successful results.

The goal of the Early Childhood Teacher Self-Reflection Model or EC-TSR is to mentor preservice teachers through professional development to self-reflect on their beliefs about parents in order to have a positive experience *when* working with parents. Engaging in professional development as it

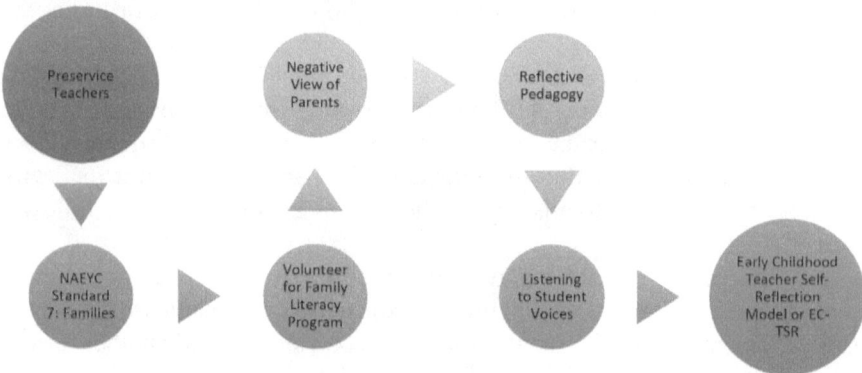

Figure 4.1   Reflexive Process BEFORE the model. *Source: Provided by author.*

relates to working with parents is important as Ferrara (2017) indicates that, "over 40 states in the U.S. have legislation in place to promote professional development in family engagement in school districts" (p. 145).

The EC-TSR Model includes six topics: (1) Getting Started, (2) Communication, (3) Cultural Awareness and Family Values, (4) Parenting Styles, (5) Learning Styles, and (6) Self-Reflection. The topics evolved as a result of listening to the preservice teachers' voices. For six weeks, in one of the teacher preparation courses, Child Growth and Development, the course instructor reserves 30 minutes of class time to discuss the weekly topic.

The topics reflect major points that need to be targeted in order to guide the preservice teachers to reflect on possible issues that may emerge from the topic while working with the parents and how to best address them. During this time the instructor shares a power point with different slides that provide examples and explanations that will help the preservice teachers understand each of the different topics of the EC-TSR Model.

Since the mentoring model involves reflection, the preservice teachers must keep a weekly reflective journal and are encouraged to provide honest answers in order to better provide guidance. Each journal entry includes one or two questions that help the preservice teacher reflect on their experiences at the family literacy project. Regardless of the topic for each week, the questions always ask the preservice teacher to reflect on their own experience as this helps develop a better understanding of others. The instructor provides comments to each of the students' weekly journals in order to scaffold their learning.

GETTING STARTED

According to Meehan and Meehan (2018), preservice teachers, "act in accordance with their beliefs when their knowledge, understanding and confidence is high (p. 1748)." Having confidence is something that preservice teachers often do not have when they first begin their teacher preparation program. The Getting Started topic is very important as it gives the students the opportunity to express their concerns and feelings.

For this topic, we want students to open up about their concerns, challenges, excitement, and expectations of working with parents, particularly working with parents who are CLD. It is also an opportunity for the mentor to explain the program or initiative in our case was the family literacy project. Once the expectations are set, it is very important that the lead mentor listen to the students even when faced with difficult opinions.

This first topic allows the mentor to listen to implicit biases that students may have about working with parents and in particular with diverse parents.

The ability to mentor preservice teachers includes learning who the students are and the experiences that shape their beliefs and perceptions. Students who are ready to listen seem to be better prepared to participate in in-depth discussions regarding parents.

The journal questions for the Getting Started topic include the following: What are your fears and concerns when thinking about working with parents? What are you most looking forward to in this project? Preservice teachers' fears and concerns may include issues of transportation or the location of the program. Since the majority of the students work they may be concerned with scheduling conflicts between the program and their workdays.

It is important that the instructor be prepared to allow the preservice teachers to voice their fears and concerns so that once those are addressed students would be better prepared to work with families. The instructor can write down those concerns so that they can be shown at the end of the professional development experience to see if the concerns are still present or if the preservice teachers have been able to overcome.

COMMUNICATION

The second topic focuses on communication. Communication is imperative for any relationship. Problems usually arise because of lack of communication or misunderstandings when trying to communicate. According to Barrat-Pugh and Maloney (2015, p. 377), communication must be "direct, prolific, streamlined and consistent" in order to effectively reach the stakeholders; in the case of the preservice teachers the stakeholders are the parents. Communication is important to learn about families, share important information and most importantly to build relationships with families.

Active communication entails the ability of the teacher to be personable and to develop positive rapport with families. When teachers express their desire to engage in communication, parents feel welcome. Teachers that have good communication with families reinforce the active participation between them, in other words, they don't only give information but they actively seek information and use the family's language and cultural practices (Berger & Riojas-Cortez, 2020).

There are different types of communication including verbal and nonverbal. Our body language is considered nonverbal communication. According to Benzer (2012), body language encompasses attitudes, feelings, and thoughts providing clues about other people and also us. Body language is largely culturally based. For example, crossing arms may be considered a sign of getting defensive or upset in the United States In some cultures, proximity is allowed while in others is considered infringement of space.

Preservice teachers must be prepared to learn and identify those differences in a positive way so that barriers to nonverbal communication can be avoided. Similarly, since verbal communication is also culturally based it is important to know the language that the parents speak, but if that is not possible then local translators should be used. This creates a sense of belonging for families as value is placed on their language. Good places to find translators include churches, universities or colleges, community centers, as well as other parents in the school.

For the topic of communication, the questions that were posed included: What changes in my communication do I need to be aware of when working with diverse parents? And, share an experience you may have had previously in communicating with parents and how this information helped you. After having a discussion regarding verbal and nonverbal communication preservice teachers may be able to determine the importance of knowing cultural norms when communicating with parents particularly if they have not had prior experience in working with diverse families.

The majority of our preservice teachers have no experience in working with parents. Our preservice teachers who do work at childcare centers or coach soccer or swimming teams have limited experience and often is not with parents of color or low-income. Preservice teachers need to also learn to communicate their thoughts and share their own ways of communicating. This will help them understand the families that they work within the family literacy program.

CULTURAL AWARENESS AND FAMILY VALUES

Although the majority of our preservice teachers are Latino, not all share the same experiences as the *Latino* parents with whom they are expected to work. Furthermore, not all families that participate in the family literacy program are of Latino descent. We have a large group of families who are immigrants and refugees from various countries. Being aware of diversity is of utmost importance in particular to successfully work with families. Cultural awareness is having the knowledge about values, beliefs, and notions of a culture including our own and these need to be taught at an early age (Sarraj et al., 2015).

Although it is important to be aware of traditions within cultures it is imperative *not* to focus on the culture from a "tourist" perspective but rather from an understanding where those traditions emerged and why they are important. Having cultural awareness means that the preservice teachers need to find out about the families' funds of knowledge. As Moll et al. (1992, p. 132) define funds of knowledge as "the skills and knowledge that have been historically and culturally developed to enable an individual or household to function within a given culture."

The topic of cultural awareness and family values is one of the most difficult one as everyone has different perceptions of the importance of culture in education and different views on family values. Family values are included in this topic as they will vary even when families are from similar ethnic background. Values include the principles that people live by examples include honesty, respect, humility, and work ethic, among others.

The preservice teachers' journal questions included for this topic are: In what ways did this experience increase your awareness of cross-cultural diversity in the classroom? What can you incorporate right away in your next lesson? These questions allow the preservice teachers not only to reflect on the type of knowledge that they need to have regarding cultural awareness but also on the kinds of strategies that they can use as the family literacy program develops.

PARENTING STYLES

Parenting styles is not something that is often discussed in teacher preparation programs unless preservice teachers take a course about working with parents. Parenting styles include the behavior and interactions that parents have with their children (Laukkanen Ojansuu et al., 2013). The way that parents "parent" has a tremendous impact on children's development (Xiaowei & Jing, 2017). This is where we often hear teachers make comments about what parents are and are not doing. Such comments, however, can damage the parent-teacher relationship.

The styles of parenting have been listed as authoritative, authoritarian, laissez-faire, and dysfunctional these styles were identified originally by Diane Baumrid (1971). When discussing parenting styles, it is important to understand the positive and negative aspects of each and show how not to prejudge parents. Just as important is to know that parenting style is also culturally based. Different cultures have different ways of parenting and must be respected. We must be careful as educators not to miss red flags of child abuse.

Many of our students are also parents and are able to see themselves in each role—parent/teacher, which seems to help them be more understanding. The model's reflection questions for this category allow preservice teachers to do an in-depth analysis beginning with their own experiences. The questions include the following: What kinds of parenting style did you grow up with in the home? How did that parenting style affect you in school? How might your own experience help you see your future students' experience?

These questions allow the preservice teachers to reflect on pros and cons so that their understanding evolves in order to be prepared to see other's experiences with their own parents.

LEARNING STYLES

Everyone has different ways of learning and that is often referred to as learning style. Teachers acknowledge that children have different learning styles and adjust the mode of instruction that will help children be more effective (Pashler et al., 2008). Brown (2000) identified the following styles:

- Kinesthetic (physical learning),
- Spatial (visual),
- Auditory (sound, listening), and
- Verbal (linguistic).

Parents also have their preferred learning style. It is important for preservice teachers to know how to provide variety of opportunities when communicating with parents in order to better create partnerships. Learning styles are important not only when developing workshops for parents, but also for effective communication.

The journal questions for the topic of learning styles include the following: What is your own learning style? What different learning styles did you notice about the parents and the children? How can you bring those differences together in the classroom? These questions should help the preservice teacher to learn about learning styles and find out good ways to use that knowledge to discover the parents' and children's learning styles in order to have a better partnership.

SELF-REFLECTION

We decided to have self-reflection at the end of the family literacy project in order for the preservice teachers to think about their experience in working with families in a holistic manner. Although this category was left to the end, the instructor encouraged self-reflection throughout the project and in the class discussions. The practice of self-reflection is imperative for preservice teachers if we want them to become what Boyd and Noblit (2015) refer to as "critically minded individuals" (p. 442). This means that preservice teachers can examine their background and determine the inequities that they have experienced (Boyd & Noblit, 2015).

By examining their own experiences, the preservice teachers can then identify the experiences of families and hopefully be willing and ready to create better educational opportunities including enhancing parent-teacher relationships. The questions for this category included: What did you learn about yourself, children, parents, and families based on your experience? How does your experience relate to what you might do as a teacher? Would you volunteer again? Explain. The open-ended questions help preservice teachers reflect on different experiences they had with the families and children. Instructor's model and guide students in discussion by sharing own experiences.

CONCLUSION AND RECOMMENDATIONS

Developing a model that helps in the training or preparation of teachers contributes to the consistency of a teacher preparation program and/or professional development endeavor particularly if the model is based on existing standards or guidelines as it provides the content needed for the preservice teachers to be knowledgeable of expectations. A model that is based on reflective pedagogy supports the belief of the importance of the view of the learner as an active participant. Providing varied platforms for reflection allows the preservice teachers to feel safe and comfortable with their thoughts and ideas while providing the instructor the opportunity to guide and mentor.

Mentoring preservice teachers is crucial to develop confidence when working with parents. The EC-TSR Model allows preservice teachers to engage in self-reflection in a weekly basis while experiencing working with parents. Preservice teachers must know that communication and knowledge of family and cultural values present a good way to create strong partnerships. It is imperative that the preservice teachers be prepared to understand the reality of many families by engaging in self-reflection and thus developing understanding of others.

Suggestions for Practice

In this section, we have included a few examples of assignments that could be incorporated in different courses to address the knowledge, skills, and dispositions described in this chapter.

1. Give a survey to preservice teachers about their perception of working with parents.

2. Incorporate a course on family partnerships or incorporate the topic throughout the courses offered in the teacher preparation program.
3. Create school partnerships where preservice teachers have the opportunity and honor of working with families of color.
4. Develop a model that is within the context of the teacher preparation program that can be easily incorporated through a course or professional development.

NOTE

1. Some settings do 6 weeks of the curriculum per semester.

References

INTRODUCTION

Young, J. L., Butler, B. R., Dolzhenko, I. N., & Ardrey, T. N. (2018). Deconstructing teacher quality in urban early childhood education. *Journal of Multicultural Teacher Education*, *12*(1), 25–34.

CHAPTER 1

Achinstein, B., Ogawa, R. T., Sexton, D., & Freitas, C. (2010). Retaining teachers of Color: A pressing problem and a potential strategy for "hard-to-staff" schools. *Review of Educational Research*, *80*(1), 71–107.

Baecher, L., & Jewkes, A. M. (2014). TESOL and early childhood collaborative inquiry: Joining forces and crossing boundaries. *Journal of Early Childhood Teacher Education*, *35*(1), 39–53.

Barrueco, S., Lopez, M., Ong, C., & Lozano, P. (2012). *Assessing Spanish-English bilingual preschoolers: A guide to best approaches and measures.* Baltimore, MD: Brookes.

Bialystok, E. (2011). Reshaping the mind: The benefits of bilingualism. *Canadian Journal of Experimental Psychology*, *65*(4), 229–235.

Bialystok, E., & Feng, X. (2011). Language proficiency and its implications for monolingual and bilingual children. In A. Y. Durunoglu & C. Goldenberg (Eds.), *Development in bilingual settings* (pp. 121–138). New York, NY: Guilford.

Bishop, R. S. (1990). Mirrors, windows, and sliding glass doors. *Perspectives*, *6*(3), ix–xi.

Burchinal, M. (2018). Measuring early care and education quality. *Child Development Perspectives*, *12*, 3–9.

Burchinal, M., Field, S., López, M. L., Howes, C., & Pianta, R. (2012). Instruction in Spanish in prekindergarten classrooms and child outcomes for English language learners. *Early Childhood Research Quarterly, 27,* 188–197.

Castro, D. C., Espinosa, L. M., & Paez, M. M. (2011). Defining and measuring quality in early education practices that promote dual language learners' development and learning. In M. Zaslow, I. Martinez-Beck, K. Tout, & H. Halle (Eds.), *Quality measurement in early childhood settings* (pp. 257–280). Baltimore, MD: Brookes.

Castro, D. C., Gillanders, C., Franco, X., Bryant, D. M., Zepeda, M., Willoughby, M. T., & Méndez, L. I. (2017). Early education of dual language learners: An efficacy study of the Nuestros Niños School Readiness Professional Development Program. *Early Childhood Research Quarterly, 40,* 188–203.

Conboy, B. (2013). Neuroscience research: How experience with one or multiple languages affects the developing brain. In Govenor's State Advisory Council on Early Learning and Care Sacramento (Ed.), *California's best practices for young dual language learners research overview papers* (pp. 1–50). Sacramento, CA: California Department of Education.

Espinosa, L. M. (2013). *Early education for dual language learners: Promoting school readiness and school success.* Washington, D.C.: Migration Policy Institute. Retrieved from: https://www.migrationpolicy.org/research/early-education-dual-language-learners-promoting-school-readiness-and-early-school-success

Espinosa, L. M. (2015). *Getting right for young children from diverse backgrounds: Applying research to improve practices with a focus on dual language learners.* New York, NY: Pearson.

Espinosa, L. M., & Calderón, M. (2015). *State early learning and development standards/guidelines, policies and related practices: How responsive are they to the needs of young dual language learners.* Greenboro, NC: The BUILD Initiative. Retrieved from: https://buildinitiative.org/Portals/0/Uploads/Documents/BuildDLLReport2015.pdf

Espinosa, L. M., & Gutiérrez-Clellan, V. (2013). *Assessment of young dual language learners in preschool.* California's best practices for dual language learners: Research overview papers.

Espinosa, L. M., & Zepeda, M. (2019). Linguistic and cultural diversity: Knowledge utilization in early care and education. In B. H. Wasik & S. Odam (Eds.), *Celebrating 50 years of child development research: Past, present, and future perspectives* (pp. 75–92). Baltimore, MD: Brookes.

Franco, X., Bryant, D. M., Gillanders, C., Castro, D. C., & Willoughby, M. (2019). Examining the linguistic interactions of dual language learners using the Language Interaction Snapshot (LISn). *Early Childhood Research Quarterly, 48,* 50–61.

García, O. (2009). Education, multilingualism and translanguaging in the 21st century. In T. Skutnabb-Kangas, R. Phillipson, A. K. Mohanty, & M. Panda (Eds.), *Social justice through multilingual education* (pp. 140–158). Bristol, UK: Multilingual Matters.

García, O., Johnson, S. I., & Seltzer, K. (2016). *The translanguaging classroom: Leveraging student bilingualism for learning.* Philadelphia, PA: Caslon Publishing.

García, O., Kleifgen, J. A., & Falchi, L. (2008). *From English language learners to emergent bilinguals. Equity Matters: Research Review 1.* The Campaign for Educational Equity. Teachers College Press.

Gay, G. (2010). *Culturally responsive teaching: Theory, research, and practice* (2nd ed.). New York, NY: Teachers College Press.

Gelatt, J., Adams, G., & Huerta, S. (2014). *Supporting immigrant families' access to prekindergarten.* Washington, D.C.: The Urban Institute. Retrieved from: https://www.urban.org/sites/default/files/publication/22286/413026-Supporting-Immigrant-Families-Access-to-Prekindergarten.PDF

Gillanders, C., Castro, D. C., & Franco, X. (2014). Learning words for life: Promoting vocabulary in dual language learners. *Reading Teacher, 68*, 213–221.

Gillanders, C., Riojas-Cortez, M., Laser, A., Miller, C., & Rudman, R. (2020). Preparing Latinx early childhood educators. *Journal of Early Childhood Teacher Education*, 1–19.

Gillanders, C., & Soltero-González, L. (2019). Discovering how writing works in different languages: Lessons from dual language learners. *Young Children, 74*(2), 32–39.

Guiberson, M. M., Barrett, K., Jancosek, E. G., & Yoshinaga-Itano, C. (2006). Language maintenance and loss in preschool-age children of Mexican immigrants. *Communication Disorders Quarterly, 28*, 4–17.

Halle, T. G., Whittaker, J. V., Zepeda, M., Rothenberg, L., Anderson, R., Daneri, P., & Buysse, V. (2014). The social–emotional development of dual language learners: Looking back at existing research and moving forward with purpose. *Early Childhood Research Quarterly, 29*(4), 734–749.

Hammer, C. S., Hoff, E., Uchikoshi, Y., Gillanders, C., Castro, D., & Sandilos, L. E. (2014). Language and literacy development of young dual language learners: A critical review. *Early Childhood Research Quarterly, 29*, 715–733.

Hardin, B. J., Lower, J. K., Smallwood, G. R., Chakravarthi, S., Li, L., & Jordan, C. (2010). Teachers, families, and communities supporting English language learners in inclusive pre-kindergartens: An evaluation of a professional development model. *Journal of Early Childhood Teacher Education, 31*(1), 20–36.

Howes, C. (2010). *Culture and child development in early childhood programs: L Practices for quality education and care.* New York: Teachers College Press.

IOM UN Migration. (2019). *Migration data portal. The bigger picture.* Retrieved from: https://migrationdataportal.org/data?i=stock_abs_&t=2019

Kovacs, A. M., & Mehler, J. (2009). Cognitive gains in 7-month-old bilingual infants. *Proceedings of the National Academy of Sciences USA, 106*(16), 6556–6560.

Landry, S. H., Assel, M. A., Carlo, M. S., Williams, J. M., Wu, W., & Montroy, J. J. (2019). The effect of the Preparing Pequeños small-group cognitive instruction program on academic and concurrent social and behavioral outcomes in young Spanish-speaking dual-language learners. *Journal of School Psychology, 73*, 1–20.

Lim, C.-I., Maxwell, K. L., Able-Boone, H., & Zimmer, C. R. (2009). Cultural and linguistic diversity in early childhood teacher preparation: The impact of contextual characteristics on coursework and práctica. *Early Childhood Research Quarterly, 24*, 64–76.

Lopez, A., Zepeda, M., Garcia, O., & Atencio, D. (2012). *Dual language learner teacher competency report.* Los Angeles, CA: Alliance for a Better Community. Retrieved from: https://buildinitiative.org/Portals/0/Uploads/Documents/DualLanguageLearnerTeacherCompetenciesReport.pdf

McCrary, D. E., Sennette, J., & Brown, D. L. (2011). Preparing early childhood teachers for English language learners. *Journal of Early Childhood Teacher Education, 32*(2), 107–117.

Moll, L. C., Amanti, C., Neff, D., & Gonzalez, N. (1992). Funds of knowledge for teaching: Using a qualitative approach to connect homes and classrooms. *Theory into Practice, 31*(2), 132–141.

Mueller, J. J., & File, N. K. (2015). Teacher preparation in changing times: One program's journey toward re-vision and revision. *Journal of Early Childhood Teacher Education, 36*(2), 175–192.

National Academies of Sciences, Engineering, and Medicine (NASEM). (2017). *Promoting the educational success of children and youth learning English: Promising futures.* Washington, D.C.: The National Academies Press. doi: 10.17226/24677

Oliva-Olsen, C., Estrada, M., & Edyburn, K. L. (2017). Preparing California's early care and education workforce to teach young Dual Language Learners. *Issues in Teacher Education, 26*, 87–113.

Paris, D. (2012). Culturally sustaining pedagogy: A needed change in stance, terminology, and practice. *Educational Researcher, 41*(3), 93–97.

Patten, E. (2016). *The nation's Latino population is defined by its youth.* Washington, D.C.: Pew Research Center.

Pew Research Center. (2019). *Key findings about U.S. immigrants.* Retrieved from: https://www.pewresearch.org/fact-tank/2019/06/17/key-findings-about-u-s-immigrants/

Poulin-Dubois, D., Blaye, A., Coutya, J., & Bialystok, E. (2011). The effects of bilingualism on toddlers' executive functioning. *Journal of Experimental Child Psychology, 108*(1), 567–579.

Pre-Kindergarten Task Force. (2017). *The current state of scientific knowledge on pre-kindergarten effects.* Chapel Hill, NC: Duke Center for Child and Family Policy. Retrieved from: https://www.brookings.edu/wpcontent/uploads/2017/04/duke_prekstudy_final_4-4-17_hires.pdf

Riojas-Cortez, M. (2001). Preschoolers' funds of knowledge displayed through sociodramatic play episodes in a bilingual classroom. *Early Childhood Education Journal, 29*(1), 35–40.

Rogoff, B. (2003). *The cultural nature of human development.* Oxford: Oxford University Press.

Samson, J. F., & Collins, B. A. (2012). *Preparing all teachers to meet the needs of English language learners: Applying research to policy and practice for teacher effectiveness.* Washington, D.C.: Center for American Progress.

Sawyer, B. E., Atkins-Burnett, S., Sandilos, L., Hammer, C. S., López, L., & Blair, C. (2018). Variations in classroom language environments of preschool children who are low-income and linguistically diverse. *Early Education and Development, 29*(3), 398–416.

Schieffiin, B. B., & Oakes, E. (1986). *Language socialization across cultures.* New York, NY: Cambridge University Press.

Sebastian-Galles, N., Albareda-Castellot, B., Weikum, W. M., & Werker, J. F. (2012). A bilingual advantage in visual language discrimination in infancy. *Psychological Science, 23*(9), 994–999.

Shanahan, T., & Lonigan, C. J. (2010). The national literacy panel: A summary of the process and the report. *Educational Researcher, 39*(4), 279–285.

Shatz, M. (1994). *A toddler's life: Becoming a person.* New York, NY: Oxford University Press.

Shrivers, E., Sanders, K., & Westbrook, T. R. (2011). Measuring culturally responsive early care and education. In M. Zaslow, I. Martinez-Beck, K. Tout, & H. Halle (Eds.), *Quality measurement in early childhood settings* (pp. 191–225). Baltimore, MD: Brookes.

Spies, T. G., Lyons, C., Huerta, M., Garza, T., & Reding, C. (2017). Beyond professional development: Factors influencing early childhood educators' beliefs and practices working with dual language learners. *Catesol Journal, 29*(1), 23–50.

Tannenbaum, M., & Berkovich, M. (2005). Family relations and language maintenance: Implications for language educational policies. *Language Policy, 4*(3), 287–309.

Valentino, R. A., & Reardon, S. F. (2015). Effectiveness of four instructional programs designed to serve English learners: Variation by ethnicity and initial English proficiency. *Educational Evaluation and Policy Analysis, 37*(4), 612–637.

Weiss, H. B., Lopez, M. E., Kreider, H., & Chatman-Nelson, C. (2014). *Preparing educators to engage families: Case studies using an ecological systems framework* (3rd ed.). Thousand Oaks, CA: SAGE.

Whyte, K. L., & Karabon, A. (2016). Transforming teacher–family relationships: Shifting roles and perceptions of home visits through the funds of knowledge approach. *Early Years, 36*(2), 207–221.

Zaslow, M., Tout, K., Halle, T., Whittaker, J. V., & Lavelle, B. (2010). *Toward the identification of features of effective professional development for early childhood educators: Literature review.* Washington, D.C.: U.S. Department of Education, Office of Planning, Evaluation and Policy Development. Retrieved from: http://www.ed.gov/about/offices/list/opepd/ppss/reports.html

Zepeda, M., Castro, D. C., & Cronin, S. (2011). Preparing early childhood teachers to work with young dual language learners. *Child Development Perspectives, 5*, 10–14.

CHAPTER 2

Berry, B., Montgomery, D., Curtis, R., Hernandez, M., Wurtzel, J., & Snyder, J. (2008). Urban teacher residencies: A new way to recruit, prepare, develop, and retain effective teachers for high-needs districts. *Voices in Urban Education, 20*, 13–23.

Brownell, M. T., Ross, D. D., Colon, E. P., & McCallum, C. L. (2005). Critical features of special education teacher preparation: A comparison with general teacher education. *The Journal of Special Education, 38*(4), 242–252.

References

Brownell, M. T., Sindelar, P. T., Kiely, M. T., & Danielson, L. C. (2010). Special education teacher quality and preparation: Exposing foundations, constructing a new model. *Exceptional Children, 7*(6), 357–377.

Early, D. M., & Winton, P. J. (2001). Preparing the workforce: Early childhood teacher preparation at 2- and 4-year institutions of higher education. *Early Childhood Research Quarterly, 16,* 285–306.

Flanigan, C. B. (2007). Preparing preservice teachers to partner with parents and communities: An analysis of college of education faculty focus groups. *The School Community Journal, 17*(2), 89–109.

Idol, L. (2006). Toward inclusion of special education students in general education. *Remedial and Special Education, 27,* 77–94.

Individuals with Disabilities Education Act, 20 U.S.C. § 1400. (2004).

Lombardi, T. P., & Hunka, N. J. (2001). Preparing general education teachers for inclusive classrooms: Assessing the process. *Teacher Education and Special Education: The Journal of Teacher Education Division of the Council for Exceptional Children, 24*(3), 183–197.

Mitchell, L. C., & Hedge, A. V. (2007). Beliefs and practices of in-service preschool teachers in inclusive settings: Implications for personnel preparation. *Journal of Early Childhood Teacher Education, 28,* 353–366.

National Center for Educational Statistics. (2017). *Children 3 to 21 years old served under Individuals with Disabilities Education Act (IDEA), Part B, by age group and sex, race/ethnicity, and type of disability: 2015–16.* U.S. Department of Education. Retrieved from: https://nces.ed.gov/programs/digest/d17/tables/dt17_204.50.asp

National Center for Educational Statistics. (2019). *The condition of education.* U.S. Department of Education. Retrieved from: https://nces.ed.gov/pubs2019/2019144.pdf

Nutter, M. E. (2011). *Teaching students with disabilities: Perception of preparedness among preservice general education teachers.* Retrieved from: ERIC (ED528050)

Obiakor, F. E., & Utley, C. A. (2004). Educating culturally diverse learners with exceptionalities: A critical analysis of the Brown case. *Peabody Journal of Education, 79*(2), 141–156.

Reese, L., Richards-Tutor, C., Hansuvadha, N., Pavri, S., & Xu, S. (2018). Teachers for inclusive, diverse urban settings. *Issues in Teacher Education, 27*(1), 17–27.

Shepherd, K. G., Fowler, S., McCormick, J., Wilson, C. L., & Morgan, D. (2016). The search for role clarity: Challenges and implications for special education teacher preparation. *Teacher Education and Special Education, 39*(2), 83–97.

Turnbull, R., Huerta, N., & Stowe, M. (2009). *The individuals with disabilities education act as amended in 2004.* Boston, MA: Pearson Education, Inc.

U.S. Department of Education, National Center for Education Statistics. (2015). *Digest of education statistics, 2013 (NCES 2015-011)*, Chapter 2. Washington, D.C.: Author.

Van Laarhoven, T. R., Munk, D. D., Lynch, K., Bosma, J., & Rouse, J. (2007). A model for preparing special and general education preservice teachers for inclusive education. *Journal of Teacher Education, 58*(5), 440–455.

Wright, E. B. (1999). Full inclusion of children with disabilities in the regular classroom: Is it the only answer? *Social Work in Education, 21*(1), 11–22.

CHAPTER 3

Apple, M., Au, W., & Gandin, L. (2010). *The Routledge international handbook of the sociology of education* (M. Apple, S. Ball, & L. Gandin, Eds.). London; New York: Routledge.

Ball, A. (2006). *Multicultural strategies for education and social change: Carriers of the touch in the US and South Africa.* New York, NY: Teacher's College.

Brown, B. (2015). *Daring greatly: How the courage to be vulnerable transforms the way we live, love, parent, and lead.* New York, NY: Avery.

Decety, J., & Jackson, P. (2004). The functional architecture of human empathy. *Behavioral and Cognitive Neuroscience Reviews, 3*(2), 71–100.

Donohue, C. (2017). *Family engagement in the digital age: Early childhood educators as media mentors.* New York, NY: Routledge.

Dotger, B. (2009). From a medicinal to educational context: Implementing a signature pedagogy for enhanced parent-teacher communication. *Journal of Education for Teaching, 35*(1), 93–94.

Epstein, J. (2011). *School, family, and community partnerships: Preparing educators and improving schools* (2nd ed.). Boulder, CO: Westview Press.

Epstein, J., & Sanders, M. (2006). Prospects for change: Preparing educators for school, family, and community partnerships. *Peabody Journal of Education, 81*(2), 81–120. doi: 10.1207/S15327930pje8102_5

Garrett, L. (2009). Parent-teacher communication: What parents and teachers think and what school leaders need to know. *Journal of School Public Relations, 30*(1), 28–50.

Giroux, H. (2004). Critical pedagogy and the postmodern/modern divide: Towards a pedagogy of democratization. *Teacher Education Quarterly, 31*(1), 31–47.

Hansen-Thomas, H., Grosso Richins, L., Kakkar, K., & Okeyo, C. (2016). I do not feel I am properly trained to help them! Rural teachers' perceptions of challenges and needs with English-language learners. *Professional Development in Education, 42*(2), 308–324. doi: 10.1080/19415257.2014.973528

Lincoln, Y., & Guba, E. (1985). *Naturalistic inquiry.* Newbury Park, CA: SAGE Publications.

McKenna, M., & Millen, J. (2013). Look! listen! learn! parent narratives and grounded theory models of parent voice, presence, and engagement in K-12 education. *School Community Journal, 23*(1), 9. Retrieved from: https://login.libweb.lib.utsa.edu/login?url=http://search.ebscohost.com/login.aspx?direct=true&db=eft&AN=91527257&scope=site

Melrose, S. (2010). Naturalistic generalization. In A. J. Mills, G. Durepos, & E. Wiebe (Eds.), *Encyclopedia of case study research.* Thousand Oaks, CA: SAGE Publications. Retrieved from: http://mr.crossref.org/iPage?doi=10.4135%2F9781412957397

Moll, L., Amanti, C., Neff, D., & Gonzalez, N. (1992). Funds of knowledge for teaching: Using a qualitative approach to connect homes and classrooms. *Theory into Practice, 31*(2), 132–141. Retrieved from: https://rylak.files.wordpress.com/2012/08/moll-et-al-1992.pdf

Nieto, S. (2009). From surviving to thriving. *Educational Leadership*, *66*(5), 8–13. Retrieved from: http://www.ascd.org/publication/educational-leadership/feb09/vol66/num05/From-Surviving-to-Thriving.aspx

Peck, N., Maude, S., & Brotherson, M. (2015). Understanding preschool teachers' perspectives on empathy: A qualitative inquiry. *Early Childhood Education Journal*, *43*(3), 169–179. doi: 10.1007/s10643-014-0648-3. Retrieved from: http://www.jstor.org.ezproxy2.library.arizona.edu/stable/4124418

Stake, R. (1995). *The art of case study research*. Thousand Oaks, CA: SAGE Publications.

Whitlock, T. (2019). *Learning to work with parents: The significance of empathy and communication in the professional development of preservice teachers* (Unpublished Doctoral dissertation). ProQuest. (13421601).

CHAPTER 4

Annamma, S., Connor, D., & Ferri, B. (2013). Dis/Ability critical race studies (DisCrit): Theorizing at the intersections of race and Dis/Ability. *Race Ethnicity and Education*, *16*(1), 1–31. doi: 10.1080/13613324.2012.730511

Apple, M., Au, W., & Gandin, L. (2010). *The Routledge international handbook of the sociology of education* (M. Apple, S. Ball, & L. Gandin, Eds.). London; New York: Routledge.

Aud, S., Hussar, W., Kena, G., Bianco, K., Frohlich, L., Kemp, J., & Tahan, K. (2011). *The condition of education 2011*. National Center for Education Statistics. Retrieved from: https://nces.ed.gov/pubs2011/2011033.pdf

Bailey, T. (2017). *Texas teacher preparation: Pathways to entering the classroom*. American Institutes for Research. Retrieved from: https://www.edtx.org/our-impact-areas/effective-teaching/texas-teacher-preparation-

Ball, A. (2006). *Multicultural strategies for education and social change: Carriers of the touch in the US and South Africa*. New York, NY: Teacher's College.

Baum, W. (2005). *Understanding behaviorism: Behavior, culture, and evolution* (2nd ed.). Malden, MA: Blackwell Publishing.

Berger, E., & Riojas-Cortez, M. (2016). *Parents as partners in education: Families and schools working together* (9th ed.). Upper Saddle River, NJ: Pearson Education.

Braun, V., & Clarke, V. (2006). Using thematic analysis in psychology. *Qualitative Research in Psychology*, *3*(2), 77–101.

Bronfenbrenner, U. (1977). Toward an experimental ecology of human development. *American Psychologist*, *32*(7), 513–531.

Brotherson, M., Summers, J., Naig, L., Kyzar, K., Friend, A., Epley, P., et al. (2010). Partnership patterns: Addressing emotional needs in early intervention. *Topics in Early Childhood Special Education*, *30*(1), 32–45.

Brown, B. (2015). *Daring greatly: How the courage to be vulnerable transforms the way we live, love, parent, and lead*. New York, NY: Avery.

Brown, J., Knoche, L., Edwards, C., & Sheridan, S. (2009). Professional development to support parent engagement: A case study of early childhood practitioners. *Early Education and Development*, *20*(3), 482–506.

References

Clarke, B. L., Sheridan, S. M., & Woods, K. E. (2010). Elements of healthy family–school relationships. In S. L. Christenson & A. L. Reschly (Eds.), *Handbook of school–family partnerships*. New York, NY: Routledge.

Creswell, J. W. (2013). *Qualitative inquiry & research design: Choosing among five approaches*. Thousand Oaks, CA: SAGE Publications, Inc.

Decety, J., & Jackson, P. (2004). The functional architecture of human empathy. *Behavioral and Cognitive Neuroscience Reviews, 3*(2), 71–100.

Delgado, R., & Stefancic, J. (2012). *Critical race theory: An introduction* (2nd ed.). New York: New York University Press.

Diaz, E., & Flores, B. (2001). Teacher as sociocultural, sociohistorical mediator. In M. Reyes & J. Halcon (Eds.), *The best for our children: Critical perspectives on literacy for Latino children* (pp. 29–47). New York: Teachers College Press.

Dillard, C. (2000). The substance of things hoped for, the evidence of things not seen: Examining an endarkened feminist epistemology in educational research and leadership. *International Journal of Qualitative Studies in Education, 13*(6), 661–681.

Donohue, C. (2017). *Family engagement in the digital age: Early childhood educators as media mentors*. New York, NY: Routledge.

Dotger, B. (2009). From a medicinal to educational context: Implementing a signature pedagogy for enhanced parent-teacher communication. *Journal of Education for Teaching, 35*(1), 93–94.

Eberly, J., Joshi, A., Konzal, J., & Galen, H. (2010). Crossing cultures: Considering ethnotheory in teacher thinking and practices. *Multicultural Education, 18*(1), 25–32.

Egbert, J., & Salsbury, T. (2009). "Out of complacency and into action": An exploration of professional development experiences in school/home literacy engagement. *Teaching Education, 20*(4), 375–393.

Eldridge, D. (2001). Parent involvement: It's worth the effort. *Young Children, 56*(4), 65–69.

Epstein, J. (2011). *School, family, and community partnerships: Preparing educators and improving schools* (2nd ed.). Boulder, CO: Westview Press.

Epstein, J., & Sanders, M. (2006). Prospects for change: Preparing educators for school, family, and community partnerships. *Peabody Journal of Education, 81*(2), 81–120.

Evans, M. (2013). Educating preservice teachers for family, school, and community engagement. *Teaching Education, 24*(2), 123–133.

Garrett, L. (2009). Parent-teacher communication: What parents and teachers think and what school leaders need to know. *Journal of School Public Relations, 30*(1), 28–50.

Gee, J. (2012, September 9). Books and games. [Webinar]. In Global Conversation in Literacy Research Web Seminar Series. Podcast retrieved from: https://www.youtube.com/watch?v=uYSJyQNW9Xc

Gerdes, K., & Segal, E. (2011). Importance of empathy for social work practice: Integrating new science. *Social Work, 56*(2), 141–148.

Giroux, H. (2004). Critical pedagogy and the postmodern/modern divide: Towards a pedagogy of democratization. *Teacher Education Quarterly, 31*(1), 31–47.

Graham-Clay, S. (2005). Communicating with parents: Strategies for teachers. *School Community Journal*, *15*(1), 117–129.

Hansen-Thomas, H., Grosso Richins, L., Kakkar, K., & Okeyo, C. (2016). I do not feel I am properly trained to help them! Rural teachers' perceptions of challenges and needs with English-language learners. *Professional Development in Education*, *42*(2), 308–324.

Leonardo, Z. (2004). Critical social theory and transformative knowledge: The functions of criticism in quality education. *Educational Researcher*, *33*(6), 11–18.

Lincoln, Y., & Guba, E. (1985). *Naturalistic inquiry*. Newbury Park, CA: SAGE.

Maude, S., Hodges, L., Brotherson, M., Hughes, K., Peck, N., Weigel, C., et al. (2009). Critical reflections on working with diverse families: Culturally responsive professional development strategies for early childhood and early childhood special educators. *Multiple Voices for Ethnically Diverse Exceptional Learners*, *12*(1), 38–53.

McAllister, G., & Irvine, J. (2002). The role of empathy in teaching culturally diverse students: A qualitative study of teachers' beliefs. *Journal of Teacher Education*, *53*(5), 433–443.

McKenna, M., & Millen, J. (2013). Look! listen! learn! parent narratives and grounded theory models of parent voice, presence, and engagement in K-12 education. *School Community Journal*, *23*(1), 9.

Mehrabian, A. (1981). *Silent messages: Implicit communication of emotions and attitudes*. Wadsworth.

Melrose, S. (2010). Naturalistic generalization. In A. J. Mills, G. Durepos, & E. Wiebe (Eds.), *Encyclopedia of case study research*. Thousand Oaks, CA: SAGE.

Merriam, S. (2009). *Qualitative research: A guide to design and implementation*. San Francisco, CA: Jossey-Bass.

Miles, M., Huberman, A., & Saldana, J. (2014). *A qualitative data analysis: A methods sourcebook* (3rd ed.). Thousand Oaks, CA: SAGE Publications.

Moll, L., Amanti, C., Neff, D., & Gonzalez, N. (1992). Funds of knowledge for teaching: Using a qualitative approach to connect homes and classrooms. *Theory into Practice*, *31*(2), 132–141.

Murray, E., McFarland-Piazza, L., & Harrison, L. (2014). Changing patterns of parent–teacher communication and parent involvement from preschool to school. *Early Child Development and Care*, *185*(7), 1031–1052.

NAEYC. (2009). *Position statement: Developmentally appropriate practice in early childhood programs serving children from birth through age 8*. Retrieved April 12, 2016, from: https://www.naeyc.org/files/naeyc/file/positions/PSDAP.pdf

Nieto, S. (2009). From surviving to thriving. *Educational Leadership*, *66*(5), 8–13.

Peck, N., Maude, S., & Brotherson, M. (2015). Understanding preschool teachers' perspectives on empathy: A qualitative inquiry. *Early Childhood Education Journal*, *43*(3), 169–179.

Schutz, A. (2006). Home is a prison in the global city: The tragic failure of school-based community engagement strategies. *Review of Educational Research*, *76*(4), 691–743.

Solorzano, D., Ceja, M., & Yosso, T. (2000). Racial microagressional, and campus racial climate: The experiences of African American college students. *The Journal of Negro Education, 69*(1/2), 60–73.

Souto-Manning, M., & Swick, K. J. (2006). Teachers' beliefs about parent and family involvement: Rethinking our family involvement paradigm. *Early Childhood Education Journal, 34*(2), 187–193.

Stake, R. (1995). *The art of case study research*. Thousand Oaks, CA: SAGE Publications.

Stake, R. (2010). *Qualitative research: Studying how things work*. New York, NY: The Guilford Press.

Symeou, L., Roussounidou, E., & Michaelides, M. (2012). "I feel much more confident now to talk with parents". An evaluation of in-service training on teacher-parent communication. *School Community Journal, 22*(1), 65.

US Census Bureau. (2017, August 28). *More than 77 million people enrolled in U.S. schools* [Press release]. Census Bureau Reports. CB17-142. Retrieved from: https://www.census.gov/newsroom/press-releases/2017/school-enrollment.html

UTSA. (2018). *UTSA future roadrunner*. Colleges & Schools. Retrieved from: https://future.utsa.edu/explore/colleges/

Van Velsor, P., & Orozco, G. (2007). Involving low-income parents in the schools: Community centric strategies for school counselors. *Professional School Counseling, 11*(1), 17–24.

Vygotsky, L. (1978). *Mind in society: The developmental of higher psychological processes*. Cambridge, MA: Harvard University Press.

Walker, J., & Dotger, B. (2012). Because wisdom can't be told: Using comparison of simulated parent-teacher conferences to assess teacher candidates' readiness for family-school partnership. *Journal of Teacher Education, 63*(1), 62.

Whitlock, T. (2019). *Learning to work with parents: The significance of empathy and communication in the professional development of preservice teachers* (Unpublished Doctoral dissertation). ProQuest. (13421601).

About the Editor and Contributors

Dr. Mari Riojas-Cortez is professor and chair of Early Childhood Studies at California State University—Channel Islands. She received her PhD from the University of Texas at Austin in Curriculum & Instruction with a concentration in Early Childhood Education and Multilingual Studies (bilingual education). Her research focuses on Latino family engagement (in early childhood contexts), young children's play in early childhood dual language settings, and early childhood teacher education. Dr. Riojas-Cortez has published in major journals including the *International Journal of Early Childhood*, the *Journal of Early Childhood Research*, the *Journal of Early Childhood Teacher Education*, the *Bilingual Research Journal*, and *Young Children*. She is coauthor of the book *Families as Partners in Education: Families and Schools Working Together* (tenth edition) and is an editor of two accepted books that focus on diversity in early childhood teacher education. Dr. Riojas-Cortez's experience with early childhood settings began in the Harlandale Independent School District in San Antonio, Texas, as a bilingual prekindergarten teacher. She has been an early childhood educator for 30 years and has worked and served in the early childhood field in different capacities. Dr. Riojas-Cortez received the Outstanding Early Childhood Teacher Educator Award in 2019 by the National Association of Early Childhood Teacher Educators and was selected as Exchange Leader by the Exchange Leadership Initiative sponsored by Childcare Exchange for her contributions to the field of early childhood education also in 2019. She served as an editor for *Dimensions of Early Childhood* for 7 years and is currently on the editorial board for the *Journal of Early Childhood Teacher Education*.

* * *

Cristina Gillanders is associate professor at the School of Education & Human Development at the University of Colorado Denver. She has been involved in the field of early childhood as a bilingual early childhood teacher, director of an early childhood program, professor, and researcher. Her research focuses on young Latinx emergent literacy, bilingualism, early childhood teaching practices for dual language learners, and minority parents' beliefs and practices related to young children's learning and development.

Allegra Montemayor has been a professional in the field of special education since 2008. Her career began as a self-contained public school teacher at an urban school district in San Antonio, Texas for students with low incidence disabilities. During her teaching career she obtained her master's degree in special education in 2010. Allegra knew early on how deep her passion was for her students with special needs and how important it was for her to be a successful educator and advocate. Thus, her interest in higher education led her to pursue a doctorate in interdisciplinary learning and teaching with a concentration in special education in 2014. Currently, she is an educational specialist for the San Antonio Independent School District (SAISD) where she oversees a district-wide alternate curriculum environment program that services students with low incidence disabilities. Additionally, she has continued her work as an adjunct instructor that has allowed her to work closely with preservice teachers and apply her knowledge, creativity, and real-world experiences into her teaching.

Tivy Nobles Whitlock, PhD, is the president of Nobles Institute. She has nearly 30 years of proven industry experience in early childhood education, technology, and professional development. She is a subject matter expert working with school age parents as young as 11 years old and grandparents who are raising young children. Dr. Whitlock's scholarly work focuses on parent engagement, strengthening teacher-parent relationships, empathic communication, and learning through play.

Karen Walker is an assistant professor and coordinator of the Child and Family Studies Program at Northwestern State University in Natchitoches, LA. She has presented at conferences locally, regionally, and internationally—including the United Kingdom, Kenya, Ireland, on the islands of Sint Maarten and Anguilla.

Marlene Zepeda is a professor emeritus in the Department of Child and Family Studies at California State University, Los Angeles. Dr. Zepeda's current scholarship focuses on workforce development and public policy initiatives to address the needs of dual language learners. Marlene received her BA in Child Development from California State University, Los Angeles, and her MA and PhD degrees in Developmental Studies and Early Childhood Education from the University of California, Los Angeles.

www.ingramcontent.com/pod-product-compliance
Lightning Source LLC
Chambersburg PA
CBHW022016300426
44117CB00005B/224